DENNING'S POINT
A Hudson River History

DENNING'S POINT

A Hudson River History

From 4000 BC to the 21st Century

Home to The Beacon Institute for Rivers and Estuaries

Jim Heron

BLACK·DOME

Black Dome Press Corp.

with

The Beacon Institute for Rivers and Estuaries

Published by
Black Dome Press Corp.
1011 Route 296
Hensonville, New York 12439
www.blackdomepress.com
Tel: (518) 734-6357

First Edition Paperback 2006
Copyright © 2006 by James Heron

Library of Congress Cataloging-in-Publication Data:

Heron, Jim.
  Denning's Point : a Hudson River history from 4000 BC to the 21st century :
home to the Beacon Institute for Rivers and Estuaries / Jim Heron. — 1st ed.
paperback.
    p. cm.
  Includes bibliographical references and index.
  ISBN-13: 978-1-883789-51-0
  ISBN-10: 1-883789-51-6
  1. Denning Point (N.Y.)—History. 2. Beacon Region (N.Y.)—History. 3. Hudson
River Valley (N.Y. and N.J.)—History, Local. I. Beacon Institute for Rivers and
Estuaries. II. Title.

  F127.D8H46 2006
  974.7'3—dc22
                            2006014286

Cover painting: *The Trading House, 1615* (detail), Len Tantillo, 1995.
Used with permission.
Cover photographs: Patricia M. Dunne. Courtesy of The Beacon Institute
  for Rivers and Estuaries.
Jim Heron photograph: Janet Hakala
Design: Toelke Associates, Chatham, NY

Printed in the USA

10 9 8 7 6 5 4 3 2 1

To Tim and Megan,

the lights in my life

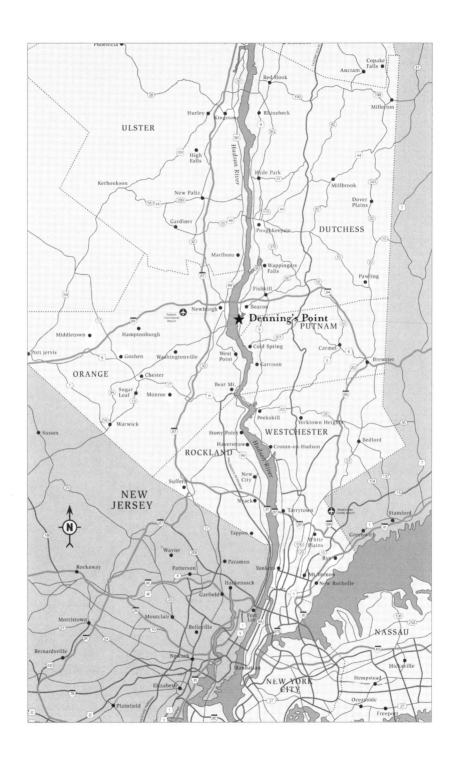

Table of Contents

Trading House, 1615 (detail), painting courtesy Len Tantillo.

FOREWORD

I like brick. I like its solidity, texture and heft, its indomitable aesthetic and longevity. I admire its testimony to human ingenuity and labor. I enjoy its mythic qualities—how earth, water and energy combine to create a building, and then a community. In fact, the alchemists' symbol for clay is a hybrid of the symbols for earth, water and oil.

Brick is a handy affection when exploring Denning's Point. Five brick structures, the remains of an old brickyard, still mark the former industrial section. Hidden piles of brick are strewn throughout the sixty-four wooded acres. A field of overgrown brick defines the Point's northwest corner. Dunes of brick form long reaches of Hudson River shore.

During the research for chapters six and seven, the rise and fall of the Denning's Point Brick Works, Jim Heron became fascinated with brick—its production, its history, its role in regional development, and in local despoilment. Much of the glory of the human-made environment in lower New York owes itself to the men and machinery that carved that later beauty out of the rich clay deposits of the Hudson River Valley.

With this in mind, I walked the Point and listened for the voices and sounds Jim describes in the pages ahead:

> I imagined entering into the midst of a functioning brickyard with all the noises of the engines, the roar of fire in the kilns, the rumble of the mixers, and the jumble of the many different languages spoken by the laborers. I imagined hearing phrases shouted by the native sons of Ireland, Hungary, Germany, Italy, Czechoslovakia, Poland and Greece.

My family's three cultures were represented in that brickyard work force; we remember our first-generation forebears, laborers all, as heroic. I am grateful for Jim's reminder that human endeavor is not only messy but honorable as well.

The cacophony of history that reverberates off the Denning's Point landscape and throughout this book is the sound of a nation's settlement and construction. From the ancient tribal occupations thousands of years before the first brick was wrought or the Point was called Denning's, to Alexander Hamilton's seminal writings on the American economy, to the land's current incarnation as a park and center for environmental knowledge, this Hudson River peninsula has embraced survival and failure, folly and success, shortsightedness and imagination.

Jim captures all this and more. He offers us the gifts of his natural teaching ability, his thousands of hours of research and writing, and, most importantly, his love of place and people.

Denning's Point still speaks in many voices. The struggle to live amidst nature, and ensure that both nature and we survive, is an enduring challenge to the human enterprise. Out of the fractured history of this spit of land can rise a new epilogue to that quest. If only we listen.

Every locale has a story to tell the world. We are blessed indeed that Denning's Point has Jim Heron as its storyteller.

John Cronin
Executive Director
The Beacon Institute for Rivers and Estuaries
May 2006

Prologue

Geologists tell us that the Appalachian Mountains are almost the oldest mountains on earth, perhaps first raised 1,000 million years ago. Much higher then, worn down to their present size by rain, ice and vegetation. They say that volcanic action pushed the Americas away from Africa and Europe, starting about 200 million years ago. Only two million years ago, they believe, we started having one ice age after another. The oceans rose and fell with each one, southern waters melted Arctic Ocean ice; then arctic winds picked up moisture, dumped billions of tons of snow in Canada and Eurasia.

They say there could have been one or two miles of ice above us here in the Hudson Valley 20,000 years ago. The last glacier went as far as Long Island, then started retreating. Oceans were lower; arctic ice returned, less snow fell.

On the way down, or melting back, glaciers occasionally left great deposits of glacial till, earth and gravel. At both Croton Point and Denning's Point they say there was enough to temporarily dam up the river, but about 13,000 years ago the ice was gone, the dams eroded, leaving only traces of rock and gravel on shores. Rivers, when they are broader and more shallow tend to leave deposits of clay, too, along the banks.

A few thousands of years ago, humans who had long settled the west coast explored all the way east. What a find! Oysters, fish, flint for their arrowheads, trees for their canoes.

Then strange pale-faced people sailed up the river with their steel tools, their thundersticks, and their square "talking leaves", their written languages.

And their strange new concept, that you could own a piece of land like you own a blanket. And you could sell it or rent it, or decide which of your children would own it after you died. Or raise the price of it.

And this extraordinary book tells a 6,000-year story of an extraordinary 64 acres on the eastern edge of the Hudson River, 60 miles north of New York City. Yes, in the Hudson Valley, that extraordinarily beautiful part of God's great green world.

Pete Seeger
Beacon, New York
April 2006

George E. Pataki, governor of the State of New York, announcing Denning's Point as the site chosen for the multimillion-dollar Rivers and Estuaries Center. Photograph by Lee Ferris, Poughkeepsie Journal. *Reprinted with permission.*

INTRODUCTION

O n April 21, 2003, George E. Pataki, governor of the State of
New York, announced the selection of Denning's Point in
Beacon, New York, as the site of the $100 million Rivers and
Estuaries Center on the Hudson River. In the planning stage since
before 2001 and with the strong support of the governor, the Rivers
and Estuaries Strategic Planning Committee developed four major
objectives for the center to pursue:

● Advance the multidisciplinary understanding of rivers
and estuaries and their associated watersheds

● Promote collaborative efforts among river and estuary
researchers and educators within the Hudson River water-
shed and globally

● Develop mechanisms for providing a scientific basis for
effective policies to guide rehabilitation, conservation, and
management of these valuable resources

● Convey to a broad audience the ecological, physical,
and social importance of rivers, estuaries, and their associated
watersheds through formal and informal education programs[1]

Over twenty other cities, towns, and villages along the Hudson
vied for the opportunity to establish this facility within their boundaries. The choice of Denning's Point in Beacon offers the best site to
fulfill these objectives. This decision was made for the right reasons,

and not for political ones: Beacon provides a waterfront with enormous ecological diversity; it is the spawning grounds for a variety of fish species; and it is located at one of the salt line transition points in the river. Furthermore, Beacon is conveniently serviced by major highways, rail lines, and an airport.

As Governor Pataki said on the day the site placement was announced, "The City of Beacon is an ideal location for studying the Hudson River." The governor summarized it best when he said the goal of the center was to be for the rivers and estuaries of the world what Woods Hole Oceanographic Institution has become for the oceans of the world. In keeping with this vision, the Rivers and Estuaries Center was incorporated as The Beacon Institute for Rivers and Estuaries in early 2006.

Evidence supports the well-informed choice for the location of The Beacon Institute on Denning's Point, but there is more wisdom in this choice than even its planners foresaw. Denning's Point is itself the "silver lining." It juts out from Beacon's western side with history dating from long before Henry Hudson made his voyage up the river that now bears his name. Denning's Point is a microcosm exemplifying the history of many of America's waterside communities. It began as a natural forest, was cultivated as rich farmland, and was nearly destroyed by industry and commerce. It now will be reborn as a carefully cared-for natural resource.

This book covers the fascinating history of Denning's Point from its resourceful Native American occupants to its intrepid, first European settlers, through its involvement in the Revolutionary War. Chapters explore the Point's rich farm years, its lavish, thirty-four-room mansion, its prosperous brickyard, and its other industries. Most importantly, however, it is about the people who lived on Denning's Point: those who worked its land, who fished from its banks, who swam off its sandy beaches, who played and picnicked on its once princely grounds, as well as those who now stand ready to restore it to vibrant good health. It is my hope that you will succumb to the enchantment of

Denning's Point as I have and that you will revel in its history and take part in its future. Discover its exciting history, as I did, with all its wonderful surprises. Decry the abuses it suffered. Delight in the glory it earned. Become familiar with the people whose lives made Denning's Point what it is — a thumbnail sketch of so many of America's riverfront communities.

Jim Heron
Project Historian
The Beacon Institute for Rivers and Estuaries
Beacon, New York
August 2006

DENNING'S POINT TIME LINE

ca. 4000 BC	Prehistoric humankind began habitation of the Point.
1609	Henry Hudson anchored off the Point.
1682	British colonial government issued a license to Francis Rombout and Gulian Verplanck to negotiate with the Native Americans for the purchase of 85,000 acres of land.
1683	Agents of Rombout and Verplanck purchased the acreage from the Native Americans for $1,250 in trade goods.
1685	The Rombout Patent (deed) was issued by Governor Thomas Dongan in the name of King James II.
1689	First map of the Rombout Patent was drawn by surveyor John Holwell.
1708	The Rombout Patent was divided into three equal parts.
1709	The Bretts take possession of Lot 1, the southern-most section of the Rombout Patent, which included the Island in Fishkill Bay, later known as Denning's Point.
1717	Roger Brett died in a boating accident; Catharyna Brett, later known as Madam Brett, took control of the family acreage.
1738	Jacobus de Peyster purchased the Island in Fishkill Bay from Madam Brett.
1780–1781	Washington, Hamilton, Lafayette, and William Denning Sr. took numerous trips from New Windsor Headquarters to troop and supply depots in Fishkill via de Peyster's Point.

April 1781	Alexander Hamilton left Washington's command and rented quarters on de Peyster's Point, where he wrote important documents.
1789	Daniel Graham purchased the Point from the de Peyster estate.
1795	Gulian Verplanck, grandson of the original purchaser of the Rombout Patent, purchased the Point from Graham.
1799	Gulian Verplanck died.
1814	The Point was conveyed to William Allen by the executors of Gulian Verplanck's estate.
1821	William Denning II purchased de Peyster's Point from William Allen; The Point was renamed Presqu'ile by Catherine Denning, but called Denning's Point by cartographers and most of the public.
1837	Martin Van Buren visited the Dennings several days before his inauguration as the eighth president of the United States.
1849	William Denning II died, leaving son William H. Denning to manage the land.
1866	William H. Denning died; management of the Point was assumed by his mother, sisters, and granddaughter.
1867	Emily Denning Van Rensselaer and Jane Denning sold two coastal strips of Denning's Point to the Boston, Hartford and Erie Railroad Company for $90,000 and held the mortgage.
1870	The Boston, Hartford, and Erie Railroad Company claimed bankruptcy; the Denning women lost two small but important parts of Denning's Point.

1872	Homer Ramsdell purchased portions of the Point at auction from the bankrupt BH & E Railroad Company.
1881	Denning's Point Brick Works began operations on the Point under the ownership of Homer Ramsdell.
1889	The last of the Denning family left the Point.
1925	David Strickland entirely updated Denning's Point Brick Works.
1939	Denning's Point Brick Words closed.
May 1942	Industrial Plants Corporation purchased Denning's Point.
Nov. 1942	Denning's Point Realty Corporation purchased Denning's Point.
1944	Anne and Marie Kriser, Virginia Danner and Doris Rosenberg jointly purchased the Point.
1947	Durisol Corporation purchased the Point and built a factory on the footprint of the brickworks.
July 1954	Durisol Corporation closed its factory on the Point.
Sept. 1954	Chestnut Cove, a holding company owned by the Griffiths family, purchased Denning's Point for the Noesting Pin Ticket Company.
1969	Noesting Pin Ticket Company assumed title of Denning's Point.
1988	The New York State Office of Parks, Recreation and Historic Preservation purchased Denning's Point for $6 million.
2003	Governor Pataki announced Denning's Point as the site choice for the Rivers and Estuaries Center.
2006	Construction began on Building One of The Beacon Institute for Rivers and Estuaries.

CHAPTER 1

In Search of
the Beginning

The fact that Native Americans occupied New York State in general, and Dutchess County in particular, for thousands of years was familiar to me. Hunting and burial grounds are situated all over Dutchess County. What I had not known was that the Island in Fishkill Bay—the first recorded name of Denning's Point—was inhabited by prehistoric humanity.[1] And so it was that the mysteries and surprises of the Point began to reveal themselves.

The first discovery was that Denning's Point had emerged from the retreating glacier of the last ice age in about 11,000 BC. While this find identified the birth date of Denning's Point, it revealed nothing about the habitation of the Point.

I was devouring all the information I could find about Native Americans in Dutchess County, but I realized that I needed to look much further into the past. Along with Native American lore, I began to read volumes of archaeology, having no idea where it was all going to lead. Then I stumbled across a headline in a 1930 edition of the *Beacon News:* "Sites of Old Indian Villages and Cemeteries Located in County; One Cemetery Found at Denning's Point."[2] This startling news meant that progress on the construction of The Beacon Institute for Rivers and Estuaries would be interrupted if Native American graves were, in fact, situated on Denning's Point. Authentic Native American burial sites are sacred and are protected. Fulfillment of multimillion-dollar dreams was at stake, but the integrity of John Cronin, then managing director of The Beacon Institute, made the next step easy. His immediate response to the discovery was: "Go find out if this is true; we have to know the truth."

The source of the allegation in the *Beacon News* was Allen Frost, then president of Vassar Brothers Institute in Poughkeepsie. Where did he get his information, and where were the artifacts, if any, stored? An exhaustive search of the elusive records of the Vassar Brothers Institute from the 1880s through the present revealed only a vague, 1948 reference to some Native American artifacts being sent to the Museum of the American Indian in New York City. This raised two more questions. Could the shipped items be the burial artifacts mentioned in the newspaper? And were these artifacts obtained

The "rickety old truck" referred to by Dr. MacCracken. Dr. Butler is sitting on the running board. Photograph courtesy of the New York State Museum, Albany, New York: A1950.03.P.001.

from a professional dig, or were they merely what the professionals term "surface pickups" from the Point? Surface pickups are insufficient as proof of regular habitation or burial sites because they may have been carried onto the site, rather than excavated from it. The *Beacon News* article gave no indication of the dating of these artifacts.

In order to investigate these questions, a trip was planned to the archives of the Museum of the American Indian, but first, all local resources needed to be exhausted.

Nearby Vassar College was the first destination, to see if the artifacts referred to in the *Beacon News* story had ended up there. This line of investigation was made under the assumption that Vassar College and Vassar Brothers Institute were connected. Alas, they have only their names in common. Nevertheless, this line of inquiry unearthed surprisingly rich pay dirt. With the help of the Vassar College archivist, I found a clear record of Native American artifacts retrieved from Denning's Point. These objects had no connection with those mentioned by the Vassar Brothers Institute, however; they were obtained from a dig conducted under the auspices of Vassar College and funded by the Carnegie Foundation during the summers of 1939 and 1940. Mary Butler, the archaeologist leading that dig, was a 1924 graduate of Vassar who had proceeded to earn a master's degree from Radcliff College and a doctorate from the University of Pennsylvania. Dr. Butler had already led two digs sponsored by the University of Pennsylvania and was working on a dig in Guatemala when Dr. Henry MacCracken, then president of Vassar College, invited her back to lead the Denning's Point expedition. Finding concrete evidence of a professionally supervised dig on the Point was extremely important and exciting.

An interesting, if condescending, view of the dig was written by Dr. MacCracken:

> In 1939 and 1940 Vassar College projected two brief surveys under the direction of Dr. Mary Butler Lewis. The workers were students from college and high school, with a few older amateurs. Thirty-eight sites were laid out and tested in the summer weeks.... There will be other digs than Dr. Mary Butler's, but none, I guess, will ever be gayer. I used to watch her ragamuffin crew, starting off in their rickety old truck, and would calculate my potential share in the resultant catastrophe. Her hard-driven scientists slept in bars and sweated out hot days in swamps and quarry slides, rock shelters and shore jungles. Folks derided them, but they sang, "Yes, we're buggy archeologists, but we don't give a hoot, It's buggy archeologists that bring home all the loot."
>
> One cache, apparently a prehistoric workshop of some humble grinder and chipper of points, was so near the highway on Bear Mountain that many got their first glimpse of the gay science of archeology, and the New York newspapers made them popular.[3]

For reasons of his own, MacCracken usually insisted on calling Dr. Butler, "Dr. Lewis," emphasizing her married name over the professional name that she clearly preferred. The correspondence between the two was icy and distinctly showed that Butler was not one with whom to trifle. This proved to be a common character trait among the pioneering women who played prominent roles in the history of Denning's Point.

Butler was not without a sense of humor, however. In one of her letters reporting on the 1939–1940 digs, she quoted the "official" Hudson Valley archaeological song:

> We are the archaeologists
> And we would have you know
> We only sink our mattocks
> Where the poison ivies grow.[4]

"The 1940 Expedition." Dr. Butler is third from the left in the bottom row. Photograph courtesy of the New York State Museum, Albany, New York: A1950.03.P.002.

Left, a Levanna projectile point; center, a Madison projectile point dating from approximately 1500 AD. They measure about three centimeters in width and two and four centimeters in length, respectively. Right: A Bare Island projectile point dating between 4000 and 3000 BC, and measuring 1.5 centimeters wide and four centimeters long. Examples of this point are also found in the Booth collection of 1905 and in the Johnson collection of 2005. Photographs by Thaddeus Beblowski. Courtesy of the New York State Museum, Albany, New York.

This poison ivy theorem was taken seriously; student diggers, quoted in that same letter said, regarding a prospective site, "It can't be any good, there's no poison ivy there."[5] To this day that remains an accurate observation about the terrain of Denning's Point—the most interesting sites are overgrown with the rash-producing impediment.

The hunt was on. The archives of Vassar College disclosed a vital clue. While the Denning's Point artifacts had at one time been displayed at Vassar College, they had accompanied Butler back to her permanent post at the University Museum of the University of Pennsylvania. I traced the artifacts from there to the Rochester Museum of Arts and Sciences, and finally to their present resting place in the New York State Museum in Albany.

The next step was, therefore, a visit to the state archives and the New York State Museum. After I had waded through the nearly one-half cubic feet of paper detailing the two summer digs led by

Left: Two Normanskill projectile points dating between 3500 and 2500 BC. Right: Axe head dating from about 2500 BC. This large artifact measures approximately fifteen centimeters long and ten centimeters at its widest point, with a groove for affixing a handle. Photographs by Thaddeus Beblowski. Courtesy of the New York State Museum, Albany, New York.

Dr. Butler, archaeology collections manager Andrea Lain rescued me and brought me into the inner sanctum of the museum. This collection storage space is right out of a set of an Indiana Jones movie. There are no windows in this huge room, which holds row after row of carefully labeled cabinets that, in turn, house tens of thousands of artifacts. This inner sanctum holds not only a great number of Denning's Point artifacts, but also a set of files containing papers and drawings detailing the locations from which Butler and her crews collected these artifacts. I took volumes of notes and was able to make a preliminary inventory of artifacts before the museum closed for the day.

Several days later I returned to the museum and its inner sanctum accompanied by Patricia Dunne, a staff member at The Beacon Institute. In another quickly passing eight hours we had the entire Denning's Point collection laid out before us on the tables within the museum's storage facility. We spent fascinating hours with the collection's experts as they educated us about the different projectile points found on Denning's Point and explained when they were most likely to have been crafted. It is hard to relay the excitement we felt when actually holding Denning's Point artifacts dating as early as 4000 BC. Most importantly, and to our great relief, we found no evidence whatever in the Butler collection indicating Native American graves on Denning's Point. The Beacon Institute project on Denning's Point looked as if it could begin to move forward again.

There was a new mystery to solve, however, before we could proceed with certainty. Among the more than one hundred Denning's Point artifacts, we found three that bore the carefully penned, unique accession numbers from the American Museum of Natural History (AMNH) in New York City. Their classification, as well as their AMNH numbering, suggested they were mistakenly filed with the Denning's Point material. A quick phone call to the museum revealed that the three artifacts in question did, indeed, come from a different site; however, Henry Booth, the collector who had presented these three items, had also donated a collection of 180 artifacts that had actually come from Denning's Point! This was an exciting discovery, especially since these artifacts were collected in the early 1880s, which was long before the Butler dig and before the advent of the brickmaking industry on the Point. We hoped that the Booth collection could tell us something about the Point's history from a perspective before the land was ravished by the brick industry. We also wondered if it were possible that the Booth artifacts were the ones referenced in the 1930 article of the *Beacon News*. With the discovery of these additional artifacts, the Native American graveyard question lingered on despite our conclusive work on the Butler artifacts.

In this day of surprises, the New York State Museum offered one more before our hunt moved to the American Museum of Natural History. Prominent books written by Arthur C. Parker in 1920[6] and by William Beauchamp in 1900[7]—archaeologists for the State of New York—mentioned the discovery by J.W. Nelson of Cold Spring of "early fireplaces and graves"[8] on Denning's Point. While numerous books and articles had alluded to Native American grave sites on Denning's Point, including the 1930 newspaper article, none gave any indication of their location on the Point or the dating of any of the artifacts found there. These two references, however, were written by well-respected archaeologists, and further investigation was needed. Quite surprisingly, it soon became obvious that the information had been directly copied from Beauchamp's book to Parker's, without any primary work to identify the artifacts of the mysterious J.W. Nelson. Whatever Nelson had uncovered seemed to have disappeared into thin air.

In the midst of our discussion with New York State Museum collection managers about these two references, one of the staff research specialists at the museum remembered a related reference in an old, unpublished manuscript. An hour or so later she returned with the goods. In this manuscript, by the same William Beauchamp noted above, we found a transcript of a letter written by J.W. Nelson dated July 31, 1889. This transcript detailed the nature and location of several Native American graves on Denning's Point.[9] While the date of the letter was 1889, the collection of the artifacts it mentioned began before 1885. This was critical information because the brickyard had started to pillage the Point of its rich clay deposits in 1881. The manuscript revealed that J.W. Nelson had visited the clay banks on the northern extreme of the Point and plucked artifacts from them as the machinery harvested the clay during the early 1880s.

We now suspected that many, if not all, of the sources noting Native American graves on Denning's Point could very well be traced back to this manuscript. One passage reads:

> The site on Denning's Point is very favorable for exploration. Excavations are being made for a sandy loam used in brick manufacture. This point extends into the river at the mouth of Mattawan creek, and is about ½ mile long, 300 to 500 yards wide. It is a site well adapted to Indian occupation.

Three heavy, long, smooth, stone pestles. The enormous size of the largest (about forty-six centimeters) and the weight of these pieces suggest a permanent settlement, because carrying them from site to site would have been burdensome. Photograph by Patricia M. Dunne. Courtesy of the American Museum of Natural History, Division of Anthropology.

About two acres at the north end have been excavated, leaving a bank from 6 to 10 feet high, extending nearly across the point; and this bank is continually receding to the south by operations of the workmen. It is in this that I have found much of interest during the last four years. Occasionally a skeleton is found, so much decayed that it is seldom a skull can be preserved. I have only two, the lower jaw of both missing.... A Pendant (gorget) is the only specimen that I am certain came from a grave 'very fine' 4 and ½ in. long, 2 and ¼ in. wide, one perforation drilled from both sides. 41 tally marks on the edges, some of them are nearly obliterated by wear and the perforation is elongated, as if from wear by suspension. Dark striped slate, with a white wavy line across its surface.[10]

Nelson carefully listed many other artifacts and noted that, as the work progressed, he no longer found any items that could be associated with Native American burial practices. We felt safe in concluding that all artifacts likely to have been burial items had been found by Nelson or destroyed shortly after the brickyard workers began excavating the Point. As with all good stories, the best part came last—Nelson's manuscript mentioned Henry Booth of Poughkeepsie and noted his earlier search yielding many surface

Seven projectile points from the Booth collection dating from 4000 BC to 1500 AD, which represents the same time span as artifacts from the Butler dig. Photograph by Patricia M. Dunne. Courtesy of the American Museum of Natural History, Division of Anthropology.

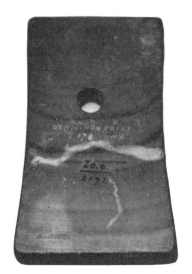

A highly polished stone pendent, most likely for ceremonial use. Photograph by Patricia M. Dunne. Courtesy of the American Museum of Natural History, Division of Anthropology.

items. Finally, the pieces of the puzzle were coming together.

The finds of the mysterious J.W. Nelson now clarified, the hunt moved to the American Museum of Natural History in New York City, and subsequently to the Museum of the American Indian, which had just been relocated to Washington, D.C. The trip to the AMNH provided corroboration of evidence of prehistoric life on Denning's Point. It also yielded information about the collector Henry Booth who had given artifacts retrieved from the Point to the museum. Together, Patricia Dunne and I examined, and she expertly photographed, the artifacts in the museum's back room, which was filled with objects not currently on display. The artifacts pictured here are samples from the AMNH collection, chosen because they are unique to the Booth collection and different from those in the Butler collection.

The AMNH archives contained papers identifying Henry Booth as a keen observer and a fastidious collector of artifacts in many parts of Dutchess County. He was not a professional archaeologist. He was a native of Poughkeepsie, New York, and known to Dr. MacCracken of Vassar College as a friend and careful collector.[11] In an undated and unpublished letter in Booth's own handwriting, he noted the following about Denning's Point:

> It has evidently been a favorite camping place of the Indian
> as the ground is very rich in relics. Some are drilled orna-
> ments, butterfly stones, etc. Two copper implements have
> been found here, small knives, made from beaten copper,
> and one piece of sheet copper, about 6 inches square, very
> much corroded, but show in two places, native silver, the
> inference is that the copper came from Lake Superior. This
> piece of copper is owned by James Nelson, the finder, who
> lives three miles east of Cold Spring, Putnam Co, on the old
> Post Road.[12]

*Pottery shards found on Denning's Point, dating either from the late Woodland
Period (1000 to 1500 AD) or the Contact Period (1500 to 1700 AD). Note the
careful tooling on many of the pieces. Photograph by Patricia M. Dunne. Courtesy
of the American Museum of Natural History, Division of Anthropology.*

The reference to James Nelson's piece of copper is extremely important, for it indicates that Nelson's findings were, at least in part, included in the Booth collection. Additionally, another careful description in the Nelson transcript precisely describes a stone tube, also shown in the AMNH pictures, including all dimensions and the broken end.[13] At the end of the day, many intriguing puzzle pieces seemed to fit together, leaving only our original question raised by the 1930 *Beacon News* reference to graves.

To settle this issue I then corresponded extensively with the staffs of the Smithsonian Institution and of the Museum of the American Indian. Continuing the wonderful cooperation that marked all my contacts with museums, the staff of the Smithsonian searched, but turned up no artifacts from Denning's Point, and the personnel at the Museum of the American Indian discovered only five. Two of the objects were on loan from the American Museum of Natural History, and none offered any new information in terms of dating habitation. Our interactions with these prominent museums, however, left us confident that we had missed nothing. My last call was to the archivist

A highly polished stone tube, probably used for ceremonial purposes. Photograph by Patricia M. Dunne. Courtesy of the American Museum of Natural History, Division of Anthropology.

from the Museum of the American Indian in search of any paperwork regarding Allen Frost, mentioned in the 1930 *Beacon News* article.

About a week later we obtained the final piece of evidence, which arrived in a packet from the archivists at the Museum of the American Indian. In copies of correspondence with Allen Frost of the Vassar Brothers Institute, they found a list of his contributions, but none of them was from Denning's Point. It appeared that Frost made his burial ground statement based only on a citation from A.C. Parker, who had lifted it from William Beauchamp, who in turn had received the previously quoted letter from J.W. Nelson of Cold Spring. With all the dots so painstakingly connected, we could assure those planning The Beacon Institute for Rivers and Estuaries that all graveyard artifacts had, indeed, been swept from the Point in the early 1880s. Work on the institute could continue, and I could begin to explore materials that would tell us more about the lives of those who lived on the Point between 4000 BC and AD 1700.

Confirmation that Denning's Point was assuredly inhabited by 4000 bc does not eliminate the possibility that there were inhabitants on the Point long before then. There is, in fact, abundant archaeological evidence that suggests earlier habitation was possible.[14] Because Denning's Point is located on a major waterway, such habitation was not only possible, but probable.

The earliest inhabitants of Denning's Point could have been Paleo-Indian hunters living between 10,000 and 7000 BC.[15] These early inhabitants followed rivers and streams inland as they hunted their food. Along trails by the banks of every major river in the northeastern United States of America, excavated projectile points date wanderers to this very early period. One of these significant trails leads northward through the Hudson Valley. How could nomads progressing along the Hudson River fail to come across these sixty-four acres of land jutting out into the river?

These early hunting expeditions were "haphazard and unrestricted wanderings of tiny groups of hunters equipped with a small inventory of chipped-stone tools," as one source described them.

"The physical appearance of these people is unknown, no skeletal remains definitely attributable to them having as yet been found."[16] Are these earliest human hunters in the Hudson Valley among the haunting memories of Denning's Point? That question remains unanswerable, for now.

Among the prehistoric peoples of the Hudson River Valley were the people from the Archaic Period, which lasted from 8000 BC through 1300 BC.[17] Theirs was a culture based on hunting, fishing, and gathering vegetation. During this time the culture evolved to one exhibiting simple social structures. Territorial distributions, tribal and probably seasonal in nature, began. Later these social units bore the names of the tribes that we know inhabited southern Dutchess County.[18] Specific projectile points commonly used in this period have been found in profusion on Denning's Point.

With the abundance of artifacts from the Archaic Period found on the Point, a clearer picture emerges of the Point's first known human occupants:

> This group can be generally described as of stocky build and medium stature (about five feet five to six inches). Their heavy boned skeletons, with strong muscular attachments, bespeak a rugged and powerful body development. Their heads, of good cranial capacity, were broad, round, and only medium height in the vault, with medium to heavy eyebrows and temporal ridges. The relatively short and wide face was characterized by a prominent lateral and anterior projection of the malars (cheekbones), medium to low orbits, and a short and broad nose.[19]

These bronzed hunters of the Archaic Period surely obtained many meals on the Point and passed over it often.

Other early Denning's Point inhabitants included the people of the Woodland Period, which is usually dated from about 1000 BC to AD 1500. Ceramics, agriculture, and settled village life developed through this era, and pottery and tools became increasingly sophisticated. Projectile points evolved to meet specific needs, and considerable trade occurred between tribal units. Evidence recovered from the Butler dig on the Denning's Point site and artifacts in the Booth collection—pieces of pottery, projectile points, and smoking pipes—proves the inhabitance of the Point throughout much of this time.

The Native Americans who inhabited Dutchess County during the Contact Period (ca. AD 1500 through AD 1700) were mostly, if not entirely, Algonkian people who had migrated from western North America following waterways northward and southward as they discovered them. These Algonkian people shared a common language, but they were not a tightly knit tribal confederacy. Algonkians were scattered throughout the Northeast and were the dominant language group from which many northeastern Native Americans can be traced. From the early to mid-1600s, they had significant contact with the European settlers from New Amsterdam (New York) to Fort Orange (Albany) along the Hudson River. They erected permanent wigwams grouped into villages. A map (shown in the next chapter) drawn in 1689 by Holwell indicates the location of several early Native American villages in Dutchess County. The Wappins (or Wappingers) tribe traveled through Pennsylvania, New Jersey, and New York, and across the Hudson River. The Wappingers occupied southwestern Dutchess County in the 1600s. The Mahicans (not to be confused with the Mohegans) migrated from the north on the eastern side of the Hudson. The Wappingers tribe subsequently joined the Mahicans, but tribal lines between the two remain unclear.[20]

The Mahicans had mastered democracy long before the American colonists implemented that form of government.[21] Ruttenber described the political structure of the Mahicans:

The government of the Mahicans was a democracy. They had a chief sachem, chosen by the nation, upon whom they look as conductor and promoter of the general welfare. This office was hereditary by the lineage of the wife of the sachem; that is, the selection of a successor, on the death of a sachem, was confined to the female branch of the family. The sachem was assisted by counselors, and also by one hero, one owl, and one runner; the rest of the nation were called young men or warriors. The sachem, or more properly king, remained at all times with his tribe and consulted their welfare; he had charge of the *mnoti*, or bag of peace, which contained the belts and strings used to establish peace and friendship with different nations, and concluded all treaties on behalf of his people.[22]

Contact between the Europeans and the Native Americans of Dutchess County during the 1600s was peaceful.[23] The indigenous people were socially and politically sophisticated, which facilitated communication with the new arrivals and played a substantial role in the talks resulting in the purchase of the Rombout Patent, which included Denning's Point.

CHAPTER 2

The Early Years

I visited the Point once again and strolled toward the most outward projection of the peninsula, where I now knew the first inhabitants had lived. As I walked along, the earliest history of the Point, which had at first confused me, now had real people attached to it. I could imagine the rustle of migrant hunters, the laughter of children around ancient campfires, the sound of a craftsman honing a point. They seemed so clean and simple, their lives not yet sullied by civilization.

By 1609, that was about to change. New voices were about to enter the story of Denning's Point. These spoke in newer tongues to the accompaniment of the slap of the rigging of their ships, the blows of their axes and hammers, and the grinding of millstones.

The first question to address now was: Who was the first European to set foot on the Point? It soon became apparent that the answer to this question was tied up in conflicting references and muddied by conjecture.

In 1609 Henry Hudson, captain of the *Half Moon*, sailed up the river that was later to bear his name. In his ship, "a mere yacht of about eighty tons burden,"[1] Hudson journeyed up the river from New Amsterdam, reaching Albany on September 19, 1609.[2] After a brief stay in Albany and considerable contact with the Native Americans, he retraced his route back down the river, deeply discouraged that he had once again failed to find a passage to the Eastern seas.[3]

On the journey back to New Amsterdam, the *Half Moon* moored mid-river between Denning's Point and Newburgh.[4] It was from this vantage point that journalist Robert Juet, a member of Hudson's crew, made the follow observation:

> At three of the clocke in the after-noone wee weighed, as soone as the ebb came, and turned downe to the edge of the mountains, on the northernmost of the mountains, and anchored; because the high land hath many points, and a narrow channel, and hath manie eddie winds. ... This is a very pleasant place to build a towne on. The road is very neere, and very good for all windes, save an east northeast wind. The mountayns look as if some metal or mineral were in them. For the trees that grow on them were all blasted, and some of them barren, with few or no trees on them.[5]

At which shore of the river Juet was looking when he made these comments is open to speculation. There can be no doubt, however, that both Juet and Hudson would have noticed the Point.

At least one local historian suggested a precise mooring location. Ruth B. Polhill, in an article entitled "Through the Years,"[6] recounted this version of the mooring:

> It was on the return trip, when the men knew that their quest for the western route to the East Indies had failed, that they were windbound one night and forced to drop anchor at the mouth of the Fishkill Creek. Curiosity and friendliness prompted the Wappingers Indians or, as Juet called them, "the copper-toned natives," to carry pumpkins, maize and tobacco out to their mysterious guests. These were gratefully accepted, and in return the Indians were given trinkets and "fire water."

If this report of the mooring location is accurate, then the woodcut named *Newburgh Bay* is incorrectly titled, for it would assuredly have been made from Denning's Point. On my next walk about the Point, I was able to identify the exact site from which the artist must have fashioned this woodcut. Could members of Hudson's crew have been the first Europeans to land on the Point? This is certainly possible, but unfortunately, unverifiable. The ship's log is silent regarding whether or not Hudson's crew actually disembarked to interact with the natives.

In 1609, when Henry Hudson viewed what is now Denning's Point, it was an island, not a peninsula.[7] The island lay so close to the mainland, however, that foot passage was probably possible at low tide. These acres were called the Island in Fishkill Bay[8] until well into the 1700s. When the Denning family took possession of the land in 1821, they added a narrow causeway of fill to allow carriage traffic onto the island. Later, industrialists expanded the job the colonists began, bringing in additional fill to widen the connector, forming a peninsula. From this time onward the tract of land experienced change by human hand, disrupting that which had stood for millennia in the delicate balance of nature.

It was almost eighty years after Hudson's voyage downriver before Europeans permanently inhabited the Beacon area in general and the Point in particular. The Dutch had built a trading house in New Amsterdam in 1614 and shortly thereafter a similar trading house in Fort Orange, but the stretch of land between the two, including Dutchess County, was not settled. While the Native Americans of the area traded extensively with the Dutch, colonists hesitated to settle in what was then a wilderness. From a European perspective, "When Westchester, Orange, and Ulster counties were settling, Dutchess County contained no inhabitants."[9] Later, the population of Dutchess County, however, would soon surpass the population of its neighbors across the river in Orange and Ulster counties.

"Newburgh Bay." Woodcut from E. M. Ruttenber's The Indian Tribes of Hudson's River to 1700.

The intriguing story of European settlement in Dutchess County and on Denning's Point began in 1683 with the creation of Dutchess County on November 1, 1683, under the rule of King Charles II of England. Under British law, the king was considered to be the source of all real property and the source of all titles to land; thus, colonial governors, acting under instructions from the king, were given the authority to issue land grants under the seal of the province. At that time, land was conveyed to a new owner by issuing a patent—a letter, similar to a present-day deed, that transferred property from one person or persons to another person or persons. By English law, the Crown considered the Native Americans to be the aboriginal owners of all land in the colonies. Prospective European owners first had to obtain a royal license to negotiate with the aboriginal owners, and then apply for a patent from the king.

Francis Rombout, "a distinguished merchant of New York,"[10] and Gulian Verplanck, his partner in the fur trade, applied for a license, which was issued on February 8, 1682. The license covered:

> All that Tract or Parcell of Land Scituate, Lyeing and being on the East side of Hudson's River, at the north side of the High Lands, Beginning from the South side of A Creek Called the fresh Kill, and by the Indians Matteawan, and from thence Northward along said Hudson's River five hundred Rodd bejond the Great Wappins Kill, called by the Indians Mawenawasigh, being the Northerly Bounds, and from thence into the Woods fouer Houers goeing. ["Fouer houers goeing" is interpreted to mean sixteen miles, the distance a man would walk normally in four hours.][11]

In terms of today's geographical boundaries, the license included the city of Beacon, the towns of Fishkill, East Fishkill, and Wappingers, about half of LaGrange, and a small piece of the town of Poughkeepsie. There is an oft-quoted legend attached to the subsequent negotiations that may be worthy of a smile, but not of belief.

According to legend, Francis Rombout offered a price for all the land he could see. Since at the time he was standing on lowlands rimmed by hills, he could not see very far. The Native Americans are said to have agreed to his terms. "Then, the story concluded, Rombout climbed a thousand feet up to the peak of Mount Beacon, viewed an immense tract and claimed it all."[12] Most historians, however, subscribe to the less exciting reports of simple negotiations between the Native Americans and the partners' agents.

Rombout and Verplanck made the purchase on August 8, 1683, after ten months of negotiations by their agents. (Neither Rombout nor Verplanck ever set foot on the land.) The plot became known as the Rombout Patent and included what is presently Denning's Point. Translated into today's language of measurement and value, the men obtained 85,000 acres for which they traded items worth about $1,250. That might seem a paltry sum to modern ears, but the amount negotiated for the Rombout Patent was roughly thirty times that paid by Pierre Minuit in 1626 for the island of Manhattan.

Given the relative values of the time, many historians feel that the Native Americans did extremely well in their negotiations and probably got the better part of the deal. They were not tricked into giving away the land; they bargained hard. Looking over the list of negotiated items, one is struck by their diversity and utility. The list from the original patent document reads:

> One hund Royalls, One hund Pound Powder, Two hund fathom of White Wampum, one hund Barrs of Lead, One hundred fathom of Black Wampum, thirty tobacco boxes ten holl adges, thirty Gunns, twenty Blankets, forty fathom of Duffils, twenty fathom of stroudwater Cloth, thirty Kittles, forty Hatchets, forty Hornes, forty Shirts, forty p stockins, twelve coates of R.Bl & b. C., ten Drawing Knives, forty earthen Juggs, forty Bottles, forty Knives, fourer ankers rum, ten halfe fatts Beere, two hund tobacco Pipes, &c., Eighty Pound Tobacco.[13]

These are all items that were valuable to the Native Americans. "Royalls" were the coin of the realm and had been used over the years in trade with the Dutch. The powder was used for hunting, and one hundred pounds was considered a huge amount. Wampum, available only in black or white, was used for trade as well as a decoration. White wampum was made from the pillar of the periwinkle seashell, which was shaped into a bead, perforated, and strung on a fiber of deer's sinew or, in later times, on linen thread. Black wampum was made from the interior portion of the common conch and was usually about double the value of its white counterpart. A fathom was the unit of measure between outstretched arms, and later became standardized at six feet. As a substitute for coin, wampum price was fixed by law. "Three purple (black) beads of wampum, or six of white, were equal to a stuyver among the Dutch, or a penny among the English."[14]

An "anker" was a cask that held approximately eight gallons of fluid, in this case rum. The "holl adges" (probably a combination of the Dutch–English words for "hollow" or "curved," and "edge") most likely referred to "adzes," tools for working wood. Stroudwater cloth was blanket material woven in Stroud, Gloucestershire, specifically for trade with Native Americans. "Duffil" referred to a tough woolen cloth with a heavy nap woven in Belgium. The items were particularly valuable to the Wappingers tribe, which led a settled village life, but would have been less useful to a warring or wandering tribe. Many of these items would not have been traded to a tribe even remotely considered an enemy by the Europeans. This well-documented negotiation speaks volumes of the shrewdness and sophistication of the Native Americans who inhabited this area.[15]

The idea that anyone could own land was totally foreign to the Native Americans. Perhaps they saw negotiations such as those around the Rombout Patent as a way to share the hunting grounds with the white man. Once negotiations had been finalized, Rombout and Verplanck applied to Thomas Dongan, British Colonial Governor of New York, for a patent, which was issued under the authority of the newly crowned King James II on

October 17, 1685. Not long afterwards the partners sold one-third of this property to Stephanus Van Cortlandt.

In 1689, surveyor John Holwell drew a map to delineate the purchase. It showed an expanse of trees north of the highlands between Fishkill Creek and Wappingers Creek, wigwams, fields and swamps, two beaver dams, waterfalls at the mouths of the creeks, and two little houses situated on the bank of Hudson at the mouth of Wappingers Creek and labeled "ye old Frenchman's."

Francis Rombout died in 1691, not long after purchasing the land and before he ever set foot on any part of his patent purchase. In his will he left to his only surviving offspring, four-year-old daughter Catharyna, his house on Broadway in New York City and his share of the land in the "Wappins." "To the fair widow Helena *née* Teller, who had been his third wife as he was her third husband, he left 4000 guilders and the ample balance of the estate."[16] Evidently Helena Rombout was displeased with his settlement to Catharyna and struck back in her own will. Helena Rombout's will allotted only nine pence to Catharyna, bequeathed five pounds to her son of her first marriage—a young man she claimed fleeced her while she was alive—and distributed the considerable remainder of her estate to her five daughters of her second marriage. To Catharyna's credit, throughout her life she refrained from reacting to her stepmother's insultingly small bequest and, instead, maintained close friendships with all her half sisters.

In 1703, at the age of sixteen, Catharyna married Roger Brett, a lieutenant in the British Navy. For the first six years of their marriage, the couple lived in the house on Broadway that Catharyna's father had willed to her. There seems little question that money was tight, given the stipulations of Rombout's will, and the Bretts began to consider the risky move to Catharyna's part of the Rombout Patent. The couple subsequently filed a friendly suit in Supreme Court in 1707 asking for a division of the Rombout Patent among the owners. A twelve-man crew of surveyors under the watchful eye of Sheriff Noxon divided the land into three, equitable parts. The

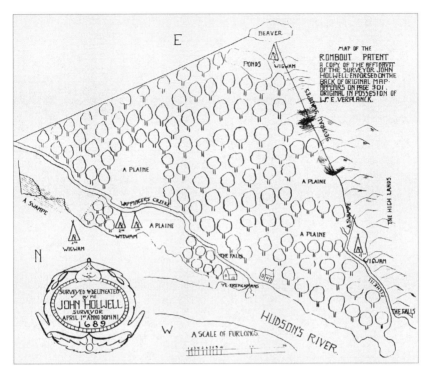

A copy of Holwell's map of 1689. The original map is in the collection of the New-York Historical Society, New York City.

Bretts obtained Lot One, which included the fertile Fishkill Valley and thus Denning's Point. Without contest from either the Verplancks or the Van Cortlandts, the court issued a writ on March 15, 1708, calling for a partition of the property. In 1709 the Bretts moved from New York City and, upon arrival in Dutchess Country, found Peter Dubois and his wife Jannetje[17] living on the Island in Fishkill Bay (Denning's Point). The Bretts made him a tenant for the remainder of his life.

The Bretts built a temporary home and a permanent gristmill at the mouth of the Fishkill Creek immediately adjacent to the Point. The mill was the only one in the area and apparently flourished, adding significantly to the otherwise thin Brett finances. Several years later the Bretts built a permanent home on the mainland, set back from the river and away from the Fishkill Creek. That homestead still stands today and is a carefully kept historic landmark within the bounds of the City of Beacon.

Catharyna and Roger Brett lived relatively uneventful lives for almost a decade. They visited their property at Denning's Point on numerous occasions. The Bretts prospered, increasing in both wealth and number; Madam Brett bore three sons during those years. One must admire the Bretts' adaptability, for this part of New York State was still wilderness. According to the first census of Dutchess County, in 1714, there were only 445 people in the whole county, including twenty-nine slaves.[18]

In 1717, Roger Brett was struck on the head by the boom of his own sloop, knocked overboard, and drowned at the mouth of the Fishkill Creek. Thus, in a heartbeat, Catharyna became sole owner of all the land within her portion of the patent. In the wake of this tragedy, Catharyna Brett became one of the region's most prominent women. Imagine the backbone it required to raise three young sons on her own in an as yet undeveloped territory occupied mostly by Native Americans.

Madam Brett, as she quickly became known, was clearly up to the challenge. Catharyna Brett was a strong and competent woman; in a very short time she developed the reputation of being a sound and tough businesswoman. In 1743 she built the Frankfort Storehouse and Freight Depot just above the Point. "This was the Colonies' first producers' cooperative, owned by 22 Dutchess County farmers. Flour ground in Madam Brett's nearby grist mill awaited shipment to New York in her fleet of sailboats. Madam Brett's masterful activities bolster the claim that she was the premier business woman of the Colonies."[19] Madam Brett took daily horseback trips to oversee the affairs of her entire lands and business ventures, which undoubtedly contributed to her success. The Point would have been included in these daily rides.

Complementing Catharyna Brett's strength was an admirable sense of fairness. She carefully ensured that the Native Americans were never driven from her land and that they continued to share the mantle of ownership. "The Wappingers Indians were allowed to remain on land which they had sold Rombout and Company, and remained on good terms until the end of her life. These same Indians were fighting with the patriots in the Revolution. A letter from Madam Brett, quoted elsewhere refers to her pledge not to disturb them. She gave this, she avers, in appreciation of a valuable service done to her."[20] Though a slaveholder—as were most Europeans with extensive landholdings in the Hudson Valley at that time—Madam Brett also exhibited consideration towards her slaves. She added the unusual stipulation to her will that slaves, if sold, had the liberty of choosing their own masters.[21]

One cannot overstate the mark made by Madam Brett during these years in Dutchess County. MacCracken, the twentieth-century historian and past president of Vassar College, later noted: "The historical records tell of a competent woman of business, unafraid to

Madam Brett's homestead, 2005. Photograph by Jim Heron.

borrow on credit, to sue or be sued, to withstand her opponents or stand by her friends; a woman generous and fair-minded, and of heroic fibre."[22] He concluded that she deserved to be remembered as the "First Lady of Dutchess."[23]

Clearly ahead of her time, Madam Brett prospered in a male-dominated world. She remained owner of Denning's Point until the death in 1737 of Peter Dubois, her tenant for life on the Point. Shortly after the death of Dubois, Madam Brett sold the Point to Jacobus de Peyster, who renamed it "de Peyster's Point." The de Peyster family maintained ownership until 1789. Jacobus de Peyster was Madam Brett's half nephew;[24] he had married one of Madam Brett's five half sisters. Considering Madam Brett's business acumen, I suspect that Jacobus de Peyster purchased the land at her request so that she might acquire more liquid assets with which to work, while retaining her virtual monopoly of the waterfront properties.

In one of the curiosities of history, nobody recorded Madam Brett's date of death. "Exactly when, how or why she died was, incredibly, not recorded. For a family that preserved her playthings and kept her business accounts and cherished her letters, it was an unimaginable oversight. Just as no one ever saved a picture or description of her, no one ever bothered to register the date and circumstances of her death."[15] Because Catharyna Brett wrote her will in late 1763 and it was proved in early 1764, most historians date her death in the spring of 1764.

History shows the establishment of several other gristmills and the growth of other forms of commerce around Denning's Point before and after Madam Brett's death. Other mentions of Denning's Point during this period are of little note. As the Revolutionary War approached, however, new research proved that Denning's Point was about to play its part in the founding of the country, leaving behind surprising stories and as-yet unexplainable mysteries.

CHAPTER 3

THE REVOLUTIONARY WAR
PERIOD

WHEN I BEGAN TO RESEARCH THE PART THAT DENNING'S POINT PLAYED IN THE UNFOLDING HISTORY OF OUR NATION, I HAD NO IDEA HOW IMPORTANT THESE SIXTY-FOUR ACRES ACTUALLY WERE. I WAS AWARE, OF COURSE, OF THE PLENTIFUL LOCAL LORE CONCERNING THE POINT'S ROLE DURING THE REVOLUTIONARY WAR. I EXPECTED TO FIND PROOF OF THE COLORFUL LEGENDS OF GENERAL WASHINGTON CROSSING THE HUDSON RIVER AND LANDING ON THE POINT AS HE TRAVELED BACK AND FORTH FROM HIS HEADQUARTERS AT NEW WINDSOR TO THE TROOPS AND SUPPLY DEPOTS AT FISHKILL LANDING AND PRESENT-DAY FISHKILL. I HAD HEARD THE STORIES OF THE FAMOUS "WASHINGTON OAKS," THE CLUSTER OF TREES UNDER WHICH WASHINGTON WAS SAID TO HAVE MOUNTED HIS HORSE ON THE POINT AFTER CROSSING THE HUDSON. I ANTICIPATED SEARCHING FOR CONCRETE PROOF OF THEIR EXISTENCE.

I WAS UNDER THE IMPRESSION, HOWEVER, THAT THE IMPORTANT EVENTS OF THE REVOLUTIONARY WAR HAPPENED AROUND THE POINT, BUT NOT ACTUALLY ON IT. THE BEACON AREA, THEN KNOWN AS FISHKILL LANDING, HOUSED MANY TROOPS AND WAS HOME TO A MAJOR SUPPLY DEPOT, BUT THE POINT ITSELF SEEMED, AT FIRST GLANCE, TO PROVIDE MERELY A LANDING PLACE. I SOON FOUND THAT, ONCE AGAIN, I HAD UNDERESTIMATED THE HISTORY OF THE POINT. AS I PROBED ITS MYSTERIES, I FOUND EVIDENCE OF HAPPENINGS ON DENNING'S POINT THAT LITERALLY CHANGED THE COURSE OF OUR NATION'S HISTORY.

T he first of many surprises surfaced with inquiries into the life of William Denning Sr. I was stunned to learn of the vital role Denning had played in the years before the Revolution, in the chaotic times during the war itself, and in the unsettled times after the Revolution.

Denning was born in Newfoundland in April 1740, and as a young boy emigrated to New York City.[1] He eventually attached himself to a mercantile firm and rose quickly within it, becoming known as a man particularly gifted in finance. In 1765 he married the boss's daughter, Sarah Hawkshurst, which surely contributed to his rise in the family business. His father-in-law was one of the most prominent and wealthy merchants in the city of New York.[2] Shortly after his marriage, Denning became increasingly active politically, shaking loose his loyalties to England and committing himself to the cause of the Colonies.

His well known views on the rights of the colonies and his open sympathy with the principles advocated by them caused him to be identified with the very first concerted movements in behalf of liberty. On the 20th of October, 1774, the delegates to the Continental Congress at Philadelphia signed, in behalf of themselves and their constituents, the "Association," or agreement, by which the colonies pledged themselves, among other things, to the non-importation and non-consumption of all articles supplied by English markets. Soon after this was done the merchants of New York, organized a Committee of Sixty which was charged the duty of "carrying into execution the Association entered into by the Continental Congress," and William Denning was elected a member thereof. [3]

Membership in the Committee of Sixty was only the beginning of a long list of important and sometimes dangerous positions for Denning. His credits, as noted in the *Biographical Directory of the American Congress*, include: "deputy of the New York Provincial Congress 1775–1777; member of the convention of State representatives in 1776 and 1777; served in the State assembly 1784–1787 and in the State Senate 1798-1808; member of the council of appointment in 1799; elected to the Eleventh Congress on March 4, 1809."[4] This is a lofty record, but it omits two very important appointments. The first appointment occurred July 19, 1776, when the Continental Congress elected Denning as one of three commissioners charged to settle the accounts of New York. The second was equally impressive. "On the 28th of April 1780, Congress paid a high compliment to his financial ability by electing him a Commissioner of the Board of Treasury. This Board was composed of five Commissioners, two of whom were members of Congress, and had entire charge of the national finances."[5]

In addition to holding these important positions, Denning enlisted in the local militia, was made a lieutenant of the 15th beat* company of the "Independents," and received his commission on September 15, 1775. Rapid promotion to the rank of captain resulted in him being known locally as "Captain Denning" and being cited thus in military correspondence of the time, as well as in the later historical records of Beacon. History makes no reference to Captain Denning as a commander of field troops, so it may be surmised that his duties were carried out solely in the areas of finance to which the Continental Congress had appointed him. Clearly, Denning is among those deserving significant note in the annals of the founding of the United States of America and not merely as one after whom a sixty-four-acre parcel of land is named.

In early 1776 Denning's first wife died, having borne him six children: five girls, three of whom died at an early age, and one boy,

---

* A "beat" company was a local militia organized by geographical boundaries such as voting precincts or counties. "Beat" is used here as one might use the term for a policeperson's beat, in this case their precinct or county. Beat companies elected their own officers and could be independent militia or become attached and under the command of the Continental Army.

William Denning II. Only their son played a large role in the unfolding history of Denning's Point. Shortly after his wife's death, Denning married her younger sister Amy, who bore him two more daughters

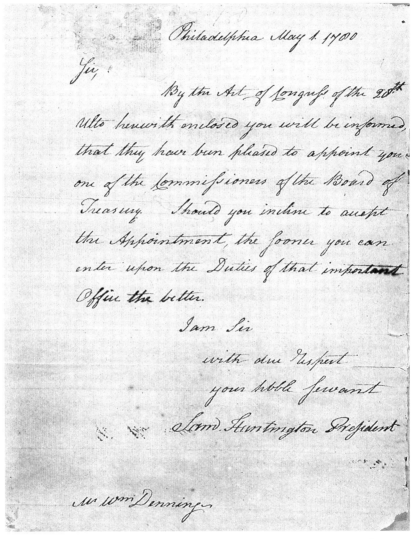

Letter from Sam Huntington, president of Congress, to William Denning informing Denning of his appointment by act of Congress to serve as a commissioner of the Board of the Treasury. Courtesy of Washington Headquarters State Historic Site, New York State Office of Parks, Recreation and Historic Preservation.

William Denning Sr. and family, painted in 1774 by William Williams in the garden of the Dennings' home on Wall Street, New York City. Photograph courtesy of the Beacon Historical Society.

and another son. Nothing is known of the fate of the daughters, but their son, Charles, died in China in 1807 while on business, leaving William Denning II as the sole surviving male and inheritor.

Before the Revolutionary War, the Denning family resided in a house on Wall Street in New York City. They maintained that property for many years during and after the war; it is the background of the family picture. Just prior to the war, William Denning Sr. purchased a country home, named Salisburgh, in the town of New Cornwall, Orange County.[6] To protect his family from the British troops occupying New York City during the War, Denning moved his entire family to Salisburgh. It was close to Newburgh and General Washington's headquarters. "The nearness of his temporary home to the headquarters of the army, and Mr. Denning's own wide acquaintance and prominence in public affairs, brought about a considerable degree of intimacy between his family and General Washington and those surrounding him."[7]

The military letters of Washington addressed to Denning show that he trusted Denning to pay the army's debts and to hold accountable those managing supplies.[8] In a letter written by Washington in 1789 to Alexander Hamilton, who was then the secretary of the treasury, he included William Denning as one of those personally selected to fill an important position in the new government.[9] Washington and Denning had more than a passing acquaintance and, in fact, spent hours together both for social and military reasons. "General and Mrs. Washington, Lafayette, Alexander and Mrs. Hamilton, were all frequent and welcome visitors to Salisburgh, where their presence graced many

William Denning as an Old Man. *Painting by John Vanderlyn.*
Courtesy of the Beacon Historical Society.

a scene of colonial hospitality."[10] Later, Denning's granddaughter Emily noted that Denning was intimate with General Washington and used to go with him often to Fishkill to review the troops.[11]

Denning and Washington frequently traveled from their headquarters in New Windsor to the Point on a horse barge. They would then leave the barge and travel inland to review troops or check the supply depots in Fishkill Landing and Fishkill. "At that day there was a ferry from New Windsor, directly to the end of the Point, and horses were brought down from the army then stationed at Fishkill, to take General Washington and Captain Denning to Fishkill."[12] On many of these journeys, William Denning II, then fourteen years of age, accompanied them. Thus, William Denning II had close knowledge of the land that he would purchase in 1821 after his father's death.

The Revolutionary War years gave rise to the legend of the Washington Oaks on the Point. The legend recounts that on his many trips from Newburgh to the troops and supply depot on the east side of the Hudson River, Washington landed near the end of the Point and secured his horse to one of two large oak trees growing along the shoreline, before re-mounting and moving inland. They became known as the "Washington Oaks." The trees are now gone, but the legend lives on with a surprising amount of historical documentation.

The April 30, 1881, edition of the *Fishkill Standard* included a trustworthy article about the oaks that suggests that the story was already old then, and it assumes its authenticity. The article stated:

> They stood like two sentinels, one on each side of the ascent by which George Washington mounted the bank as he crossed from his headquarters on the western side of the river to its eastern borders. Now the solitary survivor seems to stand, looking down mournfully at its former companion, and the wind, as it wanders through its branches, appears to whisper the sad stance, I, too wait my time to fall and mix my dust with the decay beneath.[13]

George Washington. Photograph courtesy of the Library of Congress.

The story waxed eloquently for many paragraphs describing the history of the one remaining oak. There are several other, similar articles written well before 1900.[14] One may therefore conclude that while it is unlikely that Washington himself actually slept on the Point, his horse may have.

While documenting the relationship between Denning and Washington, evidence arose of another extremely important relationship. The April 8, 1876, issue of the *Fishkill Standard* contains a transcript of a letter from Alexander Hamilton to William Denning Sr. respectfully declining an invitation to dinner. The newspaper microfilm is badly damaged, so, unfortunately, only a section of the transcript can be read, but it was enough to open a whole new line of inquiry. No mention of a relationship between Hamilton and Denning had been previously recorded by local historians or in the written history of Dutchess County. *The Papers of Alexander Hamilton* contain the original words of the letter cited in the damaged newspaper clipping.

The Washington Oaks. Photograph by John Coates Browne. Courtesy of the New-York Historical Society, New York City.

Alexander Hamilton's RSVP to William Denning declining an invitation to dinner for General Washington, Lafayette and himself. Courtesy of Washington Headquarters State Historic Site, New York State Office of Parks, Recreation and Historic Preservation.

Alexander Hamilton *by John Trumbull, 1792.*

This epistle proved to be just the tip of the iceberg in a mass of material describing a significant relationship between Hamilton and Denning. The two later served together on the board of the Bank of North America.[16] They also were elected at the same time and served together as Representatives of the General Assembly for the City and County of New York.[17] Denning opposed some of Hamilton's opinions in the New York Assembly, but did so very much in the spirit of loyal opposition.[18] Denning subsequently worked directly under Hamilton as the Commissioner for Settling Accounts of the Quartermaster Department.[19] Perhaps most telling of the nature of the relationship is the following extract from a letter sent by Denning to Hamilton:

New York, September 25, 1792.

In addressing you as an old acquaintance and a Friend you will I hope consider the Occasion as a Sufficient apology. My Son William (who has always respected and very much esteemed your person and Character) will between the first and Tenth of next month embark for Europe. His object is information and useful knowledge.... Permit me to request the favor of you Sir to Indulge him with a Line to Such person or persons in London, Paris, Holland, Germany, Russia and any other parts of Europe as you may think proper.[20]

Since Hamilton was Washington's aide-de-camp during the early years of the war, it is certain that Washington, Denning, and Hamilton must have walked together on the Point many times.

The Revolutionary War was waged around the Point, and not on it. No battles were fought on the Point. From studying a British spy map that was discovered by the colonists around 1778, however, we know that the British were very interested in the Point and that there was real potential for action there. The original map is blurred either by water damage or from having been drawn by a broad-tipped pen, but this map clearly provides three different names for this jutting piece of riverfront—Casper Prince Point, Matawhan Point, and D'Peistere Point. The spellings appear to be phonetic renditions of what the British heard locally. Casper Prince had, in fact, purchased land from the Brett family, but it was not on the Point. That mistake is understandable, especially if hearsay were the source. The British mistake in calling it Matawhan Point is explained by the Native American name for adjacent Matteawan Creek (Fishkill Creek). That name was used by the early settlers for the adjacent land, but never officially given to the Point. D'Peistere Point is an obvious corruption of de Peyster's Point, which was the correct name of the Point at the time (named after the then-current owners, the estate of Jacobus de Peyster). The incorrect spelling suggests that the British heard the name, rather than saw it written.

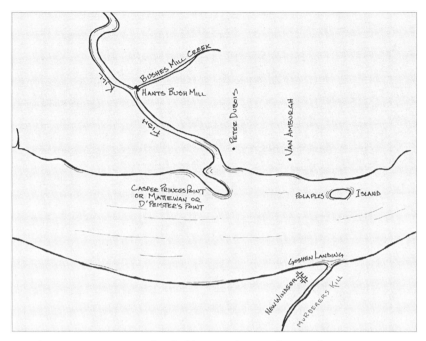

British spy map circa 1778. Sketched by Timothy David Heron from copy.

Despite the mistaken names, it is clear why the British were so interested in the Point—George Washington's comings and goings. Washington would have been vulnerable when landing on this uninhabited spit of land a mile away from busy commerce and troop deployments. The British possessed a well-disciplined army that knew how to spy, how to take advantage of weak points, and how to cripple an enemy. What a coup it would have been for the British to capture the commander of the colonial forces! If this British spy map had led to Washington's capture, it might have changed the outcome of the Revolutionary War.

Continuing to delve into the relationship between William Denning Sr. and Alexander Hamilton, I found hard evidence that influential people had engaged in important work on the Point during the Revolutionary War, including the writing of pivotal documents that shaped the Constitution. While looking for cross-

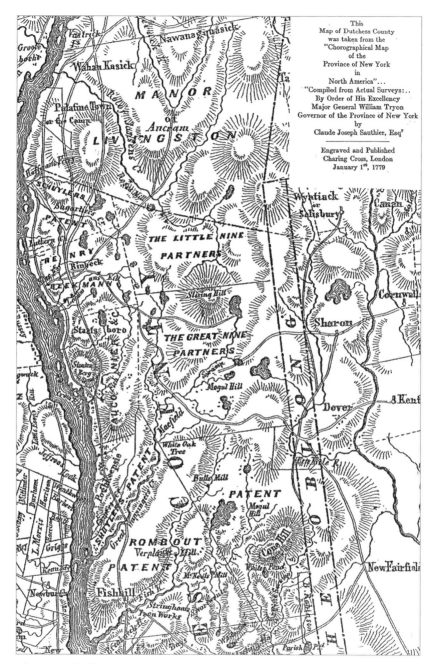

The 1779 Claude Joseph Sauthier map of Dutchess County. Note that Denning's Point (located at bottom left) is drawn pointing north, not south as is the actual case.

references between the Hamilton writings and the different names by which the Point had been known, new information came to light—six letters written in mid-1781 by Alexander Hamilton from de Peyster's Point. In addition to these letters, there were four influential editorials written by Hamilton and footnoted as having been written on de Peyster's Point.

How did Alexander Hamilton come to reside for a while on Denning's Point? Hamilton had served as Washington's aide-de-camp for four years and was eager to obtain a field command. Despite Hamilton's constant requests, however, Washington denied him the opportunity to take a field command for the probable reason that Hamilton was a superior aide-de-camp and would be extremely difficult to replace. An aide-de-camp was similar to a secretary and, as such, Hamilton penned many of Washington's letters and also deflected minor concerns from disturbing the commander in chief. In addition, Hamilton was fluent in French and invaluable in communication with the French troops and officers.

In a February 1781 letter to Phillip Schuyler, Hamilton's father-in-law and a general in the Continental Army, Hamilton described his declining relationship with Washington and the reason he had originally accepted the appointment as aide-de-camp:

> Infected with the enthusiasm of the times, an idea of the Generals character which experience soon taught me to be false overcame my scruples and induced me to accept his offer to enter into his family. I believe you know the place I held in the Generals confidence and councils of which will make it the more extraordinary to learn that for three years past I have felt no friendship for him and have professed none.[21]

The relationship between the two became increasingly fractious until Hamilton eventually left the general's staff in March of 1781. Hamilton was, however, aware of Washington's importance to the war effort and continued to defend him in public, even though he refused to work for him any longer. The friendship never recovered, although both men continued to support each other's endeavors on behalf of the newly emerging nation.

Following a trip on March 7, 1781, to review the French fleet at Newport with Washington and Lafayette, Hamilton headed to Albany to the home of his wife's family, while Washington headed for his "dreary headquarters at New Windsor."[22] This was the trip mentioned in Hamilton's letter to Denning excusing the Washingtons, Lafayette, and himself from a dinner invitation.

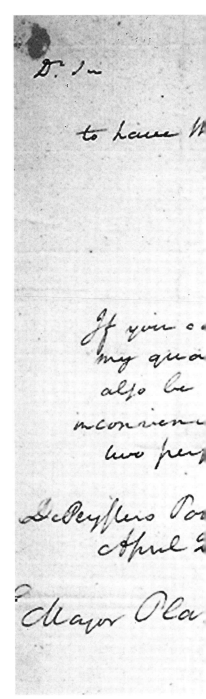

Alexander Hamilton's letter of April 28, 1781, to Major Richard Platt. Of the three business letters that Alexander Hamilton wrote while living on de Peyster' Point, this was by far the most humorous. Major Platt was a deputy quartermaster, and Hamilton was writing to him for supplies during his stay on the Point. The requests for a table, 2 small kegs, 2 a size larger, and 2 piggons (a small pail or tub with a handle) seem quite normal. The last request, however, leads to delightful speculation. It reads: "I should also be glad if it could be done without inconvenience to have a light boat which two persons could manage." This would be the boat in which Hamilton would travel almost daily across the Hudson to Washington's headquarters in order to press his case for a field command. Courtesy of the National Archives and Records Administration.

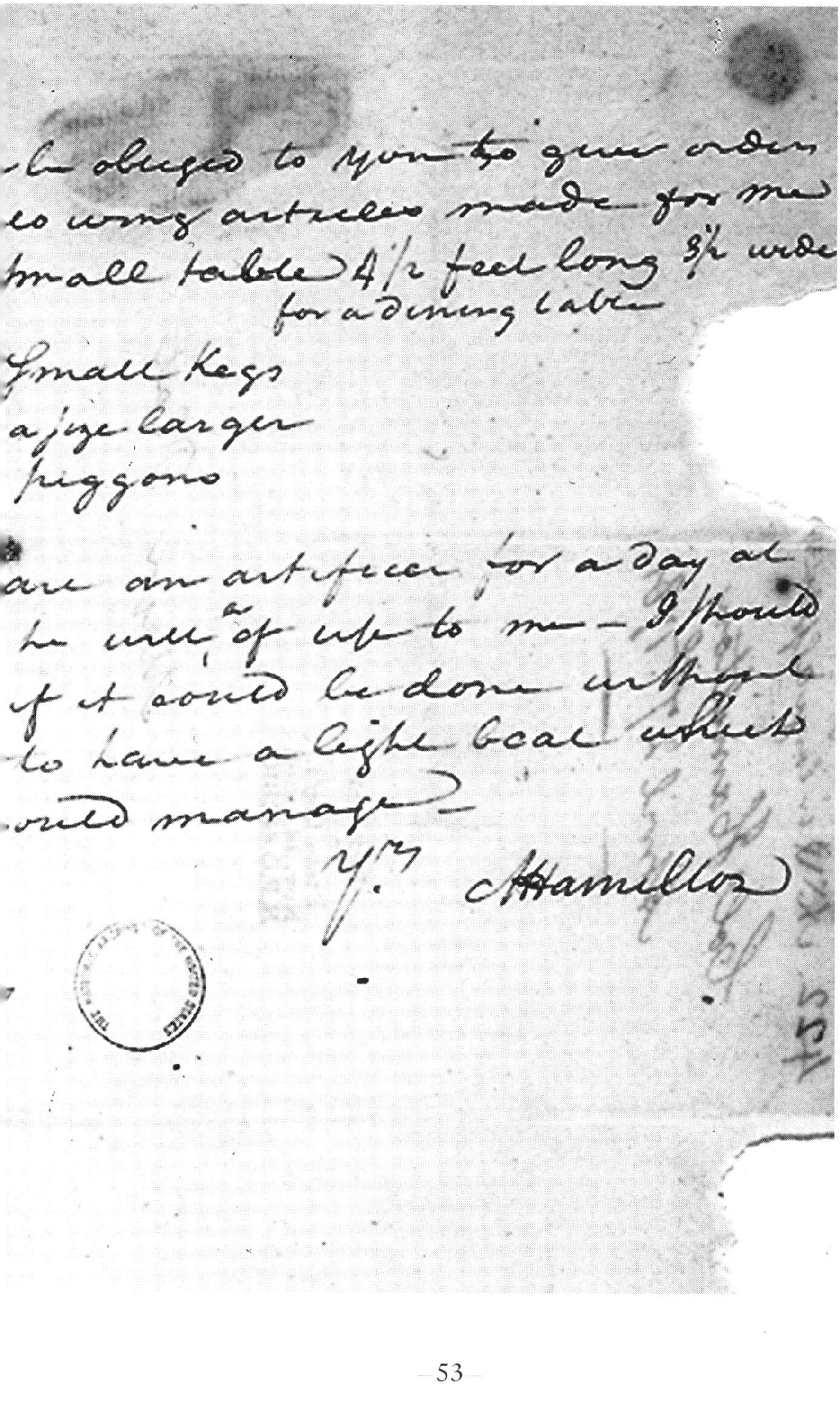

be obliged to you to give orders
to wing articles made for me
small table 4½ feet long 3½ wide
for a dining table

Small kegs
a size larger
piggons

are an artificer for a day at
the will of use to me — I should
if it could be done without
to have a light boat which
would manage —

Y.
A Hamilton

Hamilton stayed only a short time at the Schuylers' home in Albany. His continuing and burning desire for a field command position caused him to relocate with his new bride to de Peyster's Point, directly across the Hudson River from Washington's headquarters in New Windsor. From this vantage point Hamilton continued his constant badgering of Washington for a field command. (Washington by then had moved his command headquarters to the Thomas Ellison house on the banks of the Hudson River, within sight of the Point.)

Until my curiosity about exactly where Hamilton and his wife set up housekeeping on the Point drove me to additional research, there was no local information to indicate that Jacobus de Peyster, owner of the land, had done anything on the Point. Then, within Ron Chernow's new *Biography of Hamilton*, I found the answer. "In mid-April, [1781] he found quarters for himself and Eliza in a brick-and-stone Dutch dwelling at de Peyster's Point on the east bank of the Hudson, by no coincidence opposite Washington's headquarters at New Windsor."[23]

Although he had been motivated originally to move to de Peyster's Point because of its proximity to Washington, after Hamilton relocated there he began to write the aforementioned letters and editorials. As an extremely busy aide-de-camp for the previous four years, Hamilton had dedicated little time to consider other aspects of the war or possibilities for the nation he hoped would evolve after it was over. Now he set aside time for reflection and wrote an enormous amount. The serenity of the Point must have been as conducive to contemplation and creativity during Revolutionary War times as it is today.

Of the six letters that Alexander Hamilton wrote from the Point, the first three were brief business letters having to do with the war, and the next two continued his argument with Washington for a field command position. The sixth and most important letter was written to Robert Morris and is among the most important documents Hamilton ever penned. Morris had been appointed Superintendent of Finance by an act of Congress on February 20,

1781, and was, therefore, extremely influential in the newly established system of government. Hamilton's very long letter to Morris filled thirty-one pages when typeset and presented a complete system for bolstering American credit, including the necessity of founding a national bank. Most importantly Hamilton proposed a plan to restore financial order to the fledging government. "Tis by introducing order into our finances—by restoring public credit—not by gaining battles that we are finally to gain our object."[24] The letter was a work of financial genius that was produced, incredibly, by a man only in his mid-twenties. Much of our current national fiscal policy was set by Alexander Hamilton's April 30, 1781, letter to Robert Morris written from Denning's Point. A famous line from his letter reads, "A national debt, if it is not excessive, will be to us a national blessing. It will be powerful cement of our union."[25]

Hamilton's pen continued flowing in the months after producing the long letter to Morris. From de Peyster's Point in July and August of 1781, he published four editorials in consecutive issues of the *New York Packet*. This publication was from the press of Samuel Loudon, a printer who had been driven out of New York City by the British and who had set up shop in what is present-day Fishkill. The four editorials were simply named "The Continentalist, I, II, III, and IV" and were published July 12, July 19, August 9, and August 30, respectively.

In the prologue to "Continentalist IV," Hamilton first made the case to enlarge the powers of Congress. He then enumerated three recommendations that he considered necessary to "save the nation."[26] Congress, Hamilton wrote, must have the authority to regulate trade, the authority to collect a nationwide land tax, and lastly the authority to collect a moderate tax on every male above fifteen years of age. Among three additional proposals is found the basis for America's armed forces. Hamilton stated that all land and naval officers must be appointed by Congress. This provision exhibited Hamilton's desire to have the military forces all together under the control of the federal government."[27] Many of these proposals by Hamilton, all crafted on Denning's Point, are still in place today.

Hamilton wrote two additional editorials in 1782, but not from the Point. The ideas presented in the four editorials written on de Peyster's Point formed the beginning of what became the Federalist Papers and subsequently were included in the United States Constitution. The editorials laid out the groundwork for a systematic government, explained the difference between a wartime government and a peacetime government, and were the seeds of ideas expanded upon by Hamilton in his later writings. On the sixty-four acres of land that we now call Denning's Point, the kernels of the American government first sprouted.

Because of the interest generated by finding concrete evidence that Alexander Hamilton wrote important documents while he resided on the Point, efforts are now underway to locate the ruins of the house in which he lived at the time. Professional archaeologists and experts who specialize in dating old ruins will endeavor to pinpoint the exact location, which may eventually be declared a National Historic Landmark.

CHAPTER 4

The Glory Years

I made another foray onto the Point to allow all the exciting details of the Hamilton connection and the other Revolutionary War events to sink in. The Point now held a distinctively patriotic aura. As I left for home that day I wondered what other surprises might still lie in wait, and I was eager to continue my research.

In 1789, shortly after the American Revolution came to a close, the heirs of Jacobus de Peyster sold the Point to Daniel Graham. Graham made no improvements to the property and in 1795 sold the Point to Gulian Verplanck, grandson of the original purchaser of the Rombout Patent. In the peacetime America of the early 1800s, riverfront property quickly became highly desirable and, therefore, very expensive. Henry MacCracken, in his book *Blythe Dutchess*, paints a picture of waterfront properties in Dutchess County as becoming "a sort of summer White House for the presidents of railroads, shipping corporations, industries and banks."[1] Ownership of waterfront properties became a privilege of the wealthy, who brought with them the trappings of the rich, including private tutors, governesses, companions, and even riding masters.

According to MacCracken, Gulian Verplanck "worked upon his fine edition of Shakespeare, one of the first American contributions to philology"[2] while living on the waterfront. MacCracken is unclear as to whether Verplanck actually wrote while on the Point or from another waterfront property that he owned. With the death of Gulian Verplanck in 1799, de Peyster's Point was on the market. The executors of Verplanck's will had a difficult time selling the Point, despite their advertisement in the *Poughkeepsie Journal* stating that it was "the most eligible situation on Hudson's river for a gentleman's seat."[3] The wording of their advertisement suggests that this property, like all riverfront properties, had become very valuable and available only to the exceptionally wealthy.

Recorded history is silent about events occurring on the Point during the period between Gulian Verplanck's death and April 30, 1814, when the property was conveyed to William Allen, who had

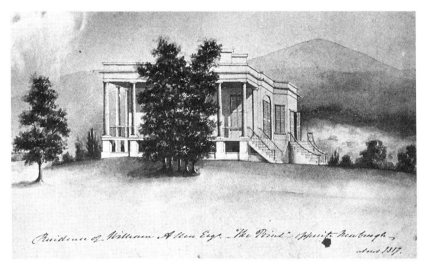

Lithograph titled "The residence of William Allen Esq. 'The Point' opposite Newburgh about 1817." Photograph courtesy of the Beacon Historical Society.

married Maria Cornelia Verplanck, the fifth of Gulian Verplanck's five daughters. William and Maria were first cousins; marriage between such close relatives was common in those times. William Allen's grandfather was the founder of Allentown, Pennsylvania, and the young gentleman was accustomed to a luxurious lifestyle. The couple built their country estate on the highest land on the Point. MacCracken noted, "The delightful Presqu'ile housed William Allen from Philadelphia and was designed quite frankly for a good time, though a Main Line sort of one."[4] MacCracken used the name "Presqu'ile" for the Point, although in Allen's time its official name was still de Peyster's Point. The new name was bestowed later, when the Denning family took possession in 1821.

The original Allen House on de Peyster's Point was a magnificent flat-roofed mansion with large porches. The family slept in the basement while living and entertaining on the first floor. The house was designed for entertaining, with a floor plan identical to that of an English hunting lodge. Legend holds that Allen and his wife "lived on such a lavish scale of elegance and hospitality that they became embarrassed financially and at the end of nine years were obliged to sell the estate."[5] Sources differ by two years as to when the Allens sold their house on de Peyster's Point. The diary of Mrs. J. R. Van Rensselaer dates the sale as occurring in 1821; MacCracken claims 1823. Because Van Rensselaer was a family member, her date may be the correct one, making the Allen sale just seven years after they obtained the property of the Point. The Denning family was in a position to buy it from the Allens in 1821 and thus to claim a place in the list of owners of the Point.

William Denning Sr., who had walked the Point with Washington and Hamilton during the Revolutionary War (with William Denning II, age fourteen, tagging along), died in 1819. He was buried in the graveyard of Saint Paul's Church on Broadway and Fulton Street, close to the New York City residence still maintained as the usual home of the Denning family. Local legend claims that Denning willed the Point to his children and grandchildren. Research into the content and intention of Denning's will reveals quite a different story, however.

The Point was not William Denning Sr.'s to leave in his will, though he did own a large part of the huge, nearby, mainland estate of Beverly Robinson, a colonel in the British Army. The Act of 1784 had appointed commissioners who were empowered to confiscate as "an act of forfeiture and sale of the estates of persons who have adhered to the enemies of the State and for declaring the sovereignty of the people of this state in respect to all property within the same."[6] Because Col. Robinson had supported Benedict Arnold, even allowing him to use his home as a headquarters at one time, it was clear Robinson remained loyal to the Crown and his lands were thus forfeit. On May 23, 1785, with the war winding down, Denning had bought a large portion of Robinson's confiscated lands as a speculation.

Denning, by his will, appointed his son, William Denning II., and his son-in-law, William Henderson, as executors of his estate. Denning ordered his executors to select one thousand prime acres from what had been the Robinson estate and to offer that acreage to all of his children on a first-refusal basis. Far from actually giving any land to his heirs, Denning's will stipulated that the highest bidder among his children would receive the land as long as the bid was not less than $30,000. Furthermore, the price was to be charged to the share of the estate belonging to the purchaser. "By a codicil, dated February 24th, 1809, William Denning devised to his executors and to Thomas Hay as trustee, one fifth of his estate for the benefit of his grandchildren, the children of his son William, and gave the trustees the same option in regard to the Beverly Farm, which he had in his will given to his children."[7] He made no stipulations as to how the proceeds set aside for his grandchildren were to be used. After Denning's death in 1819, the executors offered the Robinson land as stipulated, but there were no takers either among his children or the trustees. The executors then, as ordered by the Court of Chancery, offered the one thousand prime acres at public auction and it sold for $20,000, which was $10,000 less than what his children would have been required to pay for the property under the stipulations of Denning's will.[8] Proceeds from the sale were dispersed by the executors to Denning's children, minus the one-fifth portion set aside for his grandchildren.

Instead of opting to purchase the one thousand Robinson acres, William Denning II chose to purchase de Peyster's Point in 1821. How and when the grandchildren's portion was dispersed remains a mystery. It would seem that William Denning II had inherited his father's sound business sense, for he bought the Point for $10,000, which was $2,000 less than what William Allen had paid for it seven years before and without any apparent consideration for the house that Allen had built upon it.

Pondering this windfall for William Denning II, the pieces failed to make sense. If William Allen had built his extravagant house from scratch, the selling price of the Point should have been much higher, considering the Allens' luxurious lifestyle. If, however, there had already been a house on the site and Allen had only added to it, the price makes much better fiscal sense. Could Allen have built on the footings of the de Peyster house that Alexander Hamilton and his wife had rented? History again is silent, but the probability that there had been a house or a foundation when the Allens moved to the site increased significantly with the information regarding the selling price to William Denning II. I had no inkling at the time as to how soon that thesis would be tested.

William Denning II immediately began to make improvements on the property, including filling in enough land between the mainland and what had been an island at high tide to make a narrow causeway. Carriages could then cross to the homestead even during high tide. The improvements turned the already lovely Point into an even more valuable property consisting of rich farmland and a magnificent, accessible mansion. To these sixty-four acres Denning brought his family.

On November 3, 1794, well before his purchase of the Point, William had married Catherine Smith of Haverstraw, New York. Legend relates that Catherine's childhood years also included Revolutionary War contact with important military figures. According to the *Recollections of Presqu'ile* by Mrs. J. R. Van Rensselaer, Catherine had lived along the main road to West Point and "distinctly remembered seeing General Washington as he passed and re-passed, accompanied by his staff, when going to and returning from Head Quarters at West Point or Newburg. On one occasion she remembered seeing a party of soldiers pass, escorting a prisoner to the camp of the army at Haverstraw, to whom she handed a glass of water, as they stopped for a moment at their gate, and afterwards heard that it was Major Andre of the British Army who had been arrested as a spy near Tarrytown. Treasonable papers were found concealed about his person and he was tried, condemned and executed in the camp at Haverstraw."[9]

Denning's marriage to Catherine was a fruitful one. She bore him a son, William H., and five daughters—Caroline, Eliza, Rosette, Jane, and Emily. Rosette died in 1818 and Eliza in 1819. In 1821 the family started to spend summers on de Peyster's Point, instead of at

*Lone woman on Denning's Point circa 1860. Photograph courtesy
of the Beacon Historical Society.*

what had been the Robinson estate. Catherine renamed the Point
"Presqu'ile," which is French for "peninsula" (literally, "almost an
island"). They continued to spend winters in the family house in
New York City.

With the Denning family in summer residence and making
improvements, Presqu'ile entered into its glory years. In her diary,
William Denning II's daughter Emily, later known by her married
name, Mrs. J. R. Van Rensselaer, recounted the wonders of Presqu'ile.[10]
At the age of ten, in 1821, her first impressions were powerful and
best described in her own words: "The place was a perfect garden of
flowers, with beautiful trees shading the bank of the river and dot-
ting the lawn in front of the house. My mother gave the name of
Presqu'ile to the place, as it was almost an island, separated from the
mainland by Matteawan Creek and only connected with it by a narrow strip of ground over which ran the carriage road."[11] She added a
description of the Allen house, telling of a wing extending to the east
containing the kitchen, offices, and servants' quarters. The house

was surrounded by a colonnade on three sides, and part of the space underneath was divided into rooms and "used as sleeping accommodations for gentlemen when the number of visitors overflowed the other parts of the house."[12] In 1832 Denning added another story to the house, but retained the flat roof of an English hunting lodge.

Social life was very active on the Point, and Denning presided over innumerable events as the lord of the manor. The family summer homestead became well known throughout New York State as a place in which high society met and socialized. Local legend holds that Martin Van Buren visited the Point shortly before taking the oath of office as president of the United States in 1837. At that time in history, the president was sworn into office during the first week of March, which is still winter in the Hudson Valley and before summer houses opened for the season. The source of this legend is the diary of Emily Denning, but such a visit was unlikely, given that Presqu'ile was only habited by the Denning family during spring and

Three women on Denning's Point path. Photograph courtesy of the Beacon Historical Society.

Martin Van Buren, eighth president of the United States. Photograph courtesy of the National Park Service.

summer until 1842. The diary reference to Van Buren's visit appears in a paragraph filled with other Presqu'ile events, which adds to the confusion. While it is possible that the family opened the house early that year, it is also possible that the president-elect visited the Denning family in their New York City residence. An exhaustive search of Van Buren's papers failed to offer any conclusive evidence. The fact that Van Buren sought out William Denning II so close to his inauguration is significant to the Denning family history, but local legend claiming the Point as the meeting location remains unsubstantiated.[13]

In 1839 Emily Denning married Jacob Rutsen Van Rensselaer at Presqu'ile and returned to New York City to live with her new husband in a house of their own. In 1842 the lease expired on William Denning's New York City house and he made the decision to move the family to Presqu'ile year-round. Emily remained with her husband in New York. Four years later, in 1846, Emily's husband died unexpectedly and she moved from New York to the Point to live with her daughter, also named Emily, her sister Jane, her brother William H., and her parents. Emily's only other surviving sister, Caroline, had married and moved from the Point. William Denning II and his son William H. cleared and cultivated the land, converting it into a rich and fruitful farm.

Denning's Point farmland. Photograph courtesy of the Beacon Historical Society.

William Denning II died in 1849, leaving the entire estate to his wife Catherine and his surviving children—William, Jane, and Emily. William took over managing the family fortune and running the farm, which under his supervision continued to grow and thrive. In addition to being a talented farmer, William prospered as a merchant, as had his father and grandfather before him. An article in the June 14, 1866, *Fishkill Standard* provides a hint of his merchant status along with extraordinary details related to the sinking of one of his ships:

> Sloop Sunk—Last Thursday the sloop *Newburgh,* owned by Mr. Wm. H. Denning, and commanded by M.D. Lonsberry, of Matteawan, was sunk a short distance above Poughkeepsie, near Crum Elbow, going down so suddenly as to take with her "Black Pete," of this village, who was in the cabin at the time, preparing dinner. Capt. L. and a young man named Robert Macauley, of Newburgh, were able to save themselves by means of the small boat, which the captain had just time to detach from the sinking vessel. The sloop had a heavy deck load of flagging stone consigned to Mr. C. L. Strong, of this village, and the wind blowing very hard at the time, she careened considerable, when the stone shifted position swamping the boat suddenly. The loss will be considerable. The drowned boy, "Pete," had no relatives or near friends, to our knowledge to mourn his loss, but our citizens will miss his dwarfed shape, his peculiar physiognomy, his quaint sayings and actions. "Poor Black Pete" will long live in the memory of hundreds of persons. How old he was, where he came from, or his real name, we know not.[14]

The article also suggests that, like his father and grandfather, William exhibited no racial prejudice in the hiring of personnel. William Denning Sr. had freed his three black slaves in 1800, long before the manumission laws in New York of the 1820s and the

Emancipation Proclamation of 1863. William Denning II hired all the help he needed, both black and white, and never owned any slaves.

In 1852, shortly after the death of William Denning II, tradition bowed to practicality and a peaked roof was added to the mansion in order to stop the constant leaks resulting from having an impractical, flat roof. When the construction was complete, the house boasted thirty-four rooms and magnificent views of the Hudson River from three of its sides.

While we know little about William H.'s participation in the social events of the Point, his sister Emily's diary is filled with detailed descriptions of extravagant social affairs. Emily tells of sailboats anchored off their dock, and of rowboats, and even a barge, to take guests to Newburgh where the steamboat landed its passengers. "Our stable was always filled with horses, and large riding and driving parties would scour the country, ascend the Beacon, or make long expeditions to various points of interest on both sides of the river."[15]

Stables on Denning's Point. Photograph courtesy of the Beacon Historical Society.

Croquet on the lawn of Denning Mansion circa 1860. Photograph courtesy of the Beacon Historical Society.

Front of Denning Mansion circa 1860. Photograph by John Coates Browne. Courtesy of the New-York Historical Society, New York City.

The Denning Mansion porch circa 1860s. Photograph courtesy of the Beacon Historical Society.

View from the second story of the Denning Mansion looking west across the Hudson River. Photograph courtesy of the Beacon Historical Society.

The parlor of the Denning Mansion. Notice that the photographs on the right side of the window closest to the camera are among those in this chapter. Photograph courtesy of the Beacon Historical Society.

Tea parties were regular events and by invitation only; they were usually followed by a sumptuous meal, with guests leaving late in the evening or staying overnight. Spirits were high and life was good on Presqu'ile during the mid-1800s. Many anecdotes are recorded carefully in the *Recollections of Presqu'ile*. There are two versions of this document: a longer version, citing Mrs. J. R. Van Rensselaer as the author; and a shorter version, claiming authorship by Emily Denning Van Rensselaer. These are, of course, two names for the same person, and the shorter version, contained verbatim within the longer document, lacks only a few introductory pages of important background information. Somewhere along the historical trail someone may have edited out the introductory portion and changed the author's name to one easily recognizable as a member of the Denning family. The earlier document is used for all citations herein.

Among the detailed stories in this delightful document is one that tells of an extraordinary barge built by the Dennings. "We also

Miss Emily Denning Van Rensselaer circa 1860. Photograph by John Coates Browne. Courtesy of the New-York Historical Society, New York City.

The Zephyr *circa 1860. Photograph courtesy of the Beacon Historical Society.*

*Women on South Rocks circa 1860. Photograph courtesy of the
Beacon Historical Society.*

had a rowing club, and a six oared barge called the 'Zephyr' which was rowed by six ladies. No gentlemen were allowed on board unless they wore a cap or hood, and shawl, so as to look like a woman."[16]

Catherine, wife of William Denning II, fails to appear in any of the stories of the Point after her husband's death; all the stories are about Emily, Jane, Emily's daughter Emily, numerous invited guests, and the extended family. Catherine Smith Denning seems to be a mere shadow in the background as son, daughters, and granddaughter take the limelight.

Emily Denning Van Rensselaer recorded many slices of life on Presqu'ile that together paint an amazing picture of ease and opulence. The whole Denning clan, including cousins, second cousins, and friends of the family, were in constant attendance during the years of good fortune. Emily mentioned my own favorite spot on the Point—the South Rocks: "Further on a rock jutted out into the water, known as South Rocks, which was a favorite resort for all the young people and where they and their friends often congregated to watch the sunsets, to sing or talk, or to sit and listen quietly to the soft wash

Waterside view of Denning Cider Mill in 1855 with a boat moored beside it. Photograph courtesy of the Beacon Historical Society.

of waves as they gently rippled up upon the sandy beach."[17] While the sandy beach has been worn away by the river, the soothing lapping of the waves against the rocks continues for all to enjoy.

Emily told of an almost constant flow of guests and the careful management of their transportation from Presqu'ile to the docks in Newburgh, where steamers lay waiting to continue their passage downriver to New York City or upriver to one of the many other wealthy estates along the Hudson River on the way to Albany. Emily wrote with candor and humor:

> On one occasion while a young cousin was visiting us, she was followed to Presqu'ile by a man who had been very attentive to her but whom she had no intention of marrying. After a stormy interview in which she was firm in her refusal to be more to him than a friend, he threatened to shoot himself, hoping in this way to frighten her into consenting to be his wife, but this also had no effect, and he was obliged to depart, which he did on his own two feet, and defer his shooting to another occasion.[18]

The diary is filled with light-hearted recollections, but never mentions William's farm business or shipping interests. Was she not interested? Or was she simply oblivious to her means of support while male members of the family were still alive to attend to business concerns?

The Denning farm prospered and became famous for its cider press, which produced hundreds of barrels of cider every year from crab apples and pippins grown in abundance on the Point. A letter from William H. Denning to Hamilton Fish, then governor of the State of New York, made it clear that the press had been successfully producing apple cider since before 1850:

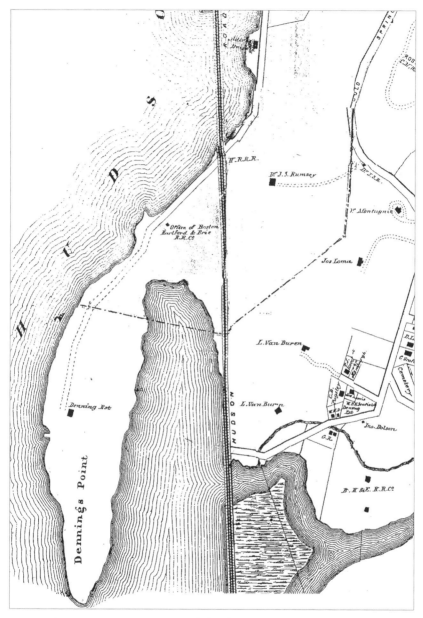

Denning's Point on an 1867 map entitled Fishkill on the Hudson *published by the* Fishkill Standard. *While railroad track plans have not yet been projected on this map, the office of the Boston, Hartford, & Erie Railroad Company is already sited near the mouth of the peninsula. Courtesy of the Beacon Historical Society.*

Fishkill Landing, December 10, 1849

Dear Sir,

I have your order form [for apple cider] of the 7th. Our crop of apples failed entirely this year owing to the heavy April frosts and we have scarcely enough for our own use. I observe, Pell advertises some in New York and it is the only place I have heard of where any can be had. The Hudson River Rail Road is in full and very successful operations as far as 7 miles above us. It is certainly the best road I have ever been on.

Yours Very Respectfully,

Wm H Denning[19]

An article in the December 7, 1872, *Fishkill Standard* also told of the mill:

One of the most famous cider manufacturing places in this county is the one of Denning's Point. For many years Denning's Crab Apple Cider has held the first place in market, and although they make large quantities, it all finds a

Denning's Point Guard dance card. Photograph by Patricia M. Dunne. Courtesy of the Beacon Historical Society.

quick sale. The cider presses are now at work, and they expect to make four hundred barrels of their famous Crab Apple Cider this year, all from apples raised on the place, not a bushel having been bought.[20]

This crab apple cider was then fermented before sale.

In the mid-1800s all cider was fermented and sold with an alcohol content that measured about half of that of most wines. It was not until refrigeration became widespread in the twentieth century that sweet cider became commercially viable. The term "hard cider" didn't come into use until the twentieth century because cider was commonly obtained fermented up until that time, which would have made the term redundant. An additional popular method of processing cider involved freezing it during the winter and reserving the alcoholic fluid that remained unfrozen. This was called applejack and measured about sixty-six proof. Thus, the Denning Cider Mill was the source of the most plentiful intoxicant available at the time. Wine and hard liquor were in very short supply and generally not obtainable by the average citizen.

The Hudson River Railroad mentioned in the letter to Hamilton Fish ran along the east shore of the river and thus along the extreme eastern edge of the Denning property. Emily's diary records the coming of the railroad with droll observation—a characteristic of many of her stories:

Our place, unlike many others situated on the river, was not injured by the building of the railroad which passed behind our point, and only crossed the narrow neck of land which connected us with the mainland. We were obliged to cross the tracks whenever we entered or left our place, but in all the long period of time in which we lived there there were some narrow escapes but we never met with a single accident from passing trains, though we crossed and re-crossed the road many times a day.[21]

What Emily's diary didn't mention was the environmental impact that railroad construction had on Denning's Point Bay. The laying of roadbed along the very fringes of the bay inhibited the free flow of water during tidal changes, and thus caused the once deep-water bay to begin filling with silt.

Farmer and merchant William H. Denning remained unmarried and spent most of his life on the Point. He kept the family fortune in good stead and remained a gentleman of substance. He served as the president of the local fire department for several years in the late 1850s. References to William H. in the newspaper suggest a friendly respect of the kind extended to local gentry: "Perhaps our friend and meteorologist, Wm. H. Denning Esq. can throw some light on why all our severe cold days come on Sunday and Monday."[22] In a later edition the *Fishkill Standard* noted:

> He was a bachelor, well educated, eccentric, of versatile mind, and abounding in humor. It seemed he spent much time in inventing something witty with which to regale the villagers on his daily visits to their stores and offices.... He made a famous cider, and in total disregard of public sentiment he insisted on placing a number of bottles annually in the parsonage cellar.[23]

The Denning family was revered in the area, for they were generous with their money as well as with their land and property. A sign of that esteem is reflected in the naming of the local militia: "Named after Mr. Denning and organized on October 10, 1859, the Denning Guard was for years the crack organization of Fishkill Landing and Matteawan. The guard had the honor of escorting the 150th N.Y.S.V.L. from Poughkeepsie to the front in the Civil War."[24] The guard first paraded on June 13, 1860, when, attired in new uniforms and led by the Newburgh Band, they drew up to the front of the Denning mansion. As William Denning appeared, the band played "Hail to the Chief"—a tune not yet reserved exclusively for the presi-

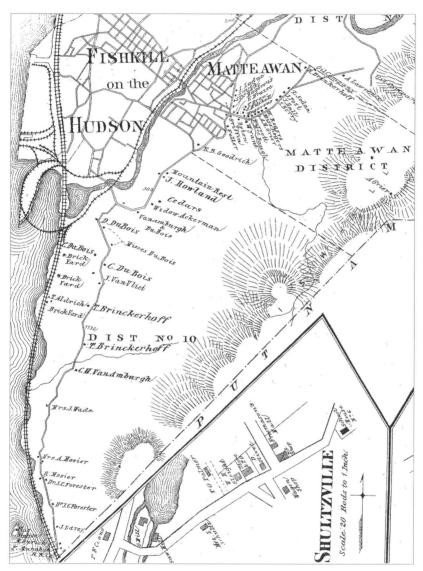

The southwest portion of an 1876 map of the border of Dutchess and Putnam counties found in the New Illustrated Atlas of Dutchess County. *Note the extraordinary railroad track plans on and around Denning's Point. If this projection had come to fruition, the entire bay from Denning's Point to Long Dock would have been filled in to form a major railroad junction. In point of fact, none of the rail lines shown west of the main line were ever constructed, and the bay remains. Courtesy of the Dutchess County Historical Society.*

dent of the United States—as a sign of affection and respect. Their new uniforms included bearskin hats and shouldered axes.[25]

> The guard was organized for more than ceremonial purposes: The Denning Guards of Fishkill Landing offered their services in a body to Gov. Morgan, and measures were instituted to form a volunteer company in that village. At a village meeting on April 22, 1861 the guard was re-organized as a battle unit. Henry Wiltsie, a young lawyer was chosen to act as the captain.[26]

On April 26, just four days later, the company left on the train for Albany and became Company C of the 18th Regiment, which enlisted for two years. There is no subsequent mention of the company in Civil War records. The only other mention of the Denning Guards discovered so far was contained in a letter written by Union soldier Richard T. Van Wyck to his mother on November 18, 1862: "I learned that the Militia Company from the [Fishkill] Landing, called the Denning Guards, are ordered to Texas."[27]

The Denning Guard continued ceremonial duties long after the Civil War had ended. An article in the October 6, 1877, *Fishkill Standard* mentioned festivities during the eighteenth anniversary of the founding of the Denning Guard.[28] The affair was formal, as is shown by the photograph of the dance card.

William H. was held in high esteem in the business world and by Civil War military personnel, as well as by the locals. There is photographic evidence of this during William H.'s tenure of business and military visitors to the peninsula now named Denning's Point. John Coates Browne, a famous photographer of the time, took a picture in October 1864 of four men on the porch of the Denning mansion near the end of the Civil War. It was a carefully composed portrait, requiring the subjects to sit absolutely still for thirty seconds. The photograph was presented by Browne to the Photographic Society of Philadelphia on April 5, 1865, and drew accolades from the press and from other photographic professionals. The

"Four Men on a Porch." Photograph by John Coates Browne. Courtesy of the New-York Historical Society, New York City.

important visitors in the photograph include General Robert Anderson and General Ambrose Burnside. Burnside is famous for his distinguished facial hair that now bears the name "side burns." While at first glance General Burnside appears to be wearing a uniform, he is actually holding a civilian top hat in his hands. At the time of the photograph, Burnside had been on furlough since August 1864, preparing his defense against the charges lodged against him by the United States Army for the disaster at the Battle of the Crater at Petersburg.[29] General Anderson, the acclaimed hero of the siege of Fort Sumter, looks exhausted and weary in the photograph. Anderson saw many battles during his time in the army. The third identifiable figure is that of William H. Denning, standing to the right and behind the seated generals. He appears to be hunched over and looks ill. This is the only photograph currently available of any male member of the original Denning family; it was taken less than two years before his death in 1866.

The identity of the fourth person in the photograph has been the source of much debate and has been narrowed to either Colonel Osborne or Gouverneur Kemble Warren. Warren was a Cold Spring resident who was relieved of his military command in 1864 and who later testified before the congressional committee reviewing the Battle of the Crater court report. Historians who argue that Colonel Osborne was the fourth person and not Warren, point out that Warren was not relieved of command until April 1, 1865, thus implying that he could not be the person in the photograph taken in 1864. A senior officer, however, often was not officially relieved of command until many months after he had already left his post for temporary duty assignments elsewhere. The fact that Warren, at the time of the photograph, had either testified or was about to testify before the congressional committee reviewing the court report regarding the Battle of the Crater in which General Burnside was involved, argues strongly that Warren is the fourth person in the photograph and that he and Burnside were at Denning's Point to discuss the case. Burnside's name was ultimately cleared, but not until after his death.

On November 1, 1866, the esteemed William H. Denning died, and with his death an important era ended. The *Fishkill Standard* of November 24, 1896, claimed: "When William H. Denning died and the halcyon days of Denning's Point seemed forever ended, the guard and the community grieved deeply. At his funeral the guard marched as escort to the remains. The hearse was flanked on either side by the company."[30] The Denning family obviously meant a good deal to the people of Fishkill Landing, and the whole community seems to have taken pride in what had become known as Denning's Point.

With all male family members now deceased, the fiscal management of the Point was taken over by Jane Denning and Emily Denning Van Rensselaer. Their mother, Catherine Smith Denning, still resided with them, but she took no part in any of the business dealings of the estate. Because none of the women had any interest

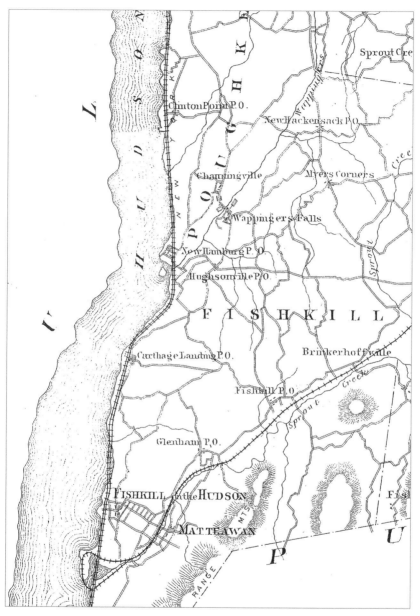

The southwest portion of an 1876 map of Dutchess County found in the New Illustrated Atlas of Dutchess County. *This map plots an excellent outline of Denning's Point, but a less than perfect portrayal of track plans. Courtesy of the Dutchess County Historical Society.*

A boy poling through the waters of the bay side of Denning's Point with a boathouse in the foreground. Notice the BH & E Railroad pilings on the left side of the picture. Photograph courtesy of the Beacon Historical Society.

in running the farm or taking part in the mercantile interests of William H., those enterprises ceased to be their means of support. Thus, the Denning women looked to other sources of income to ensure the continuation of their considerable estate.

The details of their investment strategy are found in the records of the Dutchess County Courthouse. An indenture (mortgage) held by Emily Van Rensselaer and Jane Denning from the Boston, Hartford, and Erie Railroad Company (the BH & E) was entered into the county records on November 15, 1867. The amount of the mortgage was $90,000—the equivalent of several million dollars in today's money—and represented the sale to the railroad of both coastlines

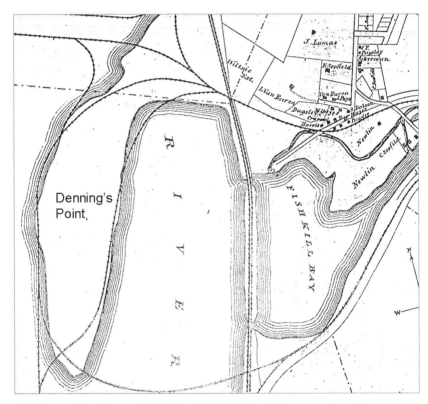

1876 map of the Boston, Hartford, and Erie Railroad Company plans for Denning's Point. Photograph courtesy of the Beacon Historical Society.

along Denning's Point. The BH & E planned to build right onto Denning's Point from two directions, with a dock at the extreme end of the Point. The mortgage was set up to pay the Dennings interest on a regular basis, and would thus provide a considerable regular income that was independent from farm produce.

Despite their need to produce investment income, it seems unlikely that the Denning women would have sold such portions of their land unless forced to do so under the threat of seizure by eminent domain. The Fifth Amendment to the Constitution defines eminent domain as the right of the government to take private property for its use by virtue of its superior dominion over the lands within its jurisdiction; that ruling had been in force since December 15, 1791. While mention of eminent domain is missing from the sources I researched, it may well have been a pressure point because the railroad was a public conveyance, even though privately owned. Note the 1876 map at left, which shows the proposed plan of the railroad on Denning's Point and makes obvious the considerable loss of privacy that the railroad's excursion would cause. So whether by fear of eminent domain or simply by poor fiscal management, a large part of Denning's Point was put at risk. The pattern of industrial encroachment was already established at the time on other riverfront properties following the building of a railroad, and the Point was on the verge of succumbing to a similar fate. The days of lavish parties on lush lands were gone forever; the decline of the glory years of Denning's Point had begun.

On August 16, 1869, at the age of ninety-nine and shortly after her daughters' sale of a portion of the Point to the BH & E Railroad Company, Catherine Smith Denning died on the Point. She had outlived her husband William by more than twenty years. There was no obituary for Catherine; a simple death notice appeared among other death notices in the *Fishkill Standard*. It read: "At Fishkill-on-Hudson, at 9 o'clock AM on the 16th Catherine Denning, widow of William Denning, deceased, in the 99th year of her age."[31] Catherine had never captured the admiration of the people of the village as had her husband, children, and grandchildren. Catherine's death in 1869 saved her the indignity of watching the decline of the Denning fortune, and with it the demise of the golden years of the Point. The future of Denning's Point now lay at the mercy of the railroad industry and subject to the machinations of an unscrupulous businessman.

CHAPTER 5

THE DECLINE AND FALL
OF THE GLORY YEARS

AFTER I CONCLUDED MY RESEARCH OF THE GOLDEN YEARS, I MADE ANOTHER EXCURSION TO THE PLACE WHERE SO MUCH HISTORY HAD UNFOLDED. AS I WALKED ACROSS THE TRACKS AND ONTO THE PENINSULA, I BECAME AWARE FOR THE FIRST TIME OF TRAVERSING THAT DISTINCT BOUNDARY BEFORE ENTERING THE POINT'S LAND. I THOUGHT OF EMILY'S DIARY COMMENTS ABOUT SEVERAL NEAR MISSES WITH THE RAILROAD OVER THE YEARS. I MADE MY WAY TO THE MANSION SITE, WHICH IS LOCATED ON THE HIGHEST PART OF THE POINT AND APPROXIMATELY TWO-THIRDS OF THE WAY TO THE END. THE MANSION IS NOW JUST RUBBLE WITH FOUR OBVIOUS CORNERS AND A TRENCH THAT SURROUNDS THE RUINS. IT IS SAD TO COMPARE THE PICTURES OF THE ONCE-PRINCELY ESTATE IN ITS PRIME TO THE PRESENT WRECKAGE. NOT ONLY THE HOUSE ITSELF, BUT THE WAY OF LIFE IT REPRESENTED IS LONG GONE. AS I STOOD IN THE HEAVY UNDERGROWTH AND BENEATH THE PIONEER TREES THAT DOT THE WHOLE CENTER OF THE POINT, I COULD ALMOST HEAR THE SOUNDS OF HORSES PULLING THE EQUIPMENT THAT WOULD HAVE BEEN PART OF A WORKING FARM DURING THE GLORY YEARS.

Part of that now-defunct farm was the cider mill that had generated income for the Denning family. It is still an impressive building, despite its crumbling walls. Debate arose over the years as to whether this building, known locally as "the cider mill," was, in fact, the site of the Denning Cider Mill, but a citation in Charles Caldwell's survey field book of Denning's Point, written in 1878, conclusively ends the debate. Caldwell, a well-known engineer and cartographer, made his home in Newburgh. He carefully located the cider mill precisely on the traditional site on the eastern shore of the Point and meticulously noted its dimensions as forty feet and six inches by eighty-one feet and six inches—the exact dimensions of the existing structure.[1] This information answers the question of location, but it does not tell us why a building so large was needed for a cider mill.

An article from the *Fishkill Standard* solved that mystery. "After careful 'racking' from barrel to barrel, the cider generated effervescence and some alcohol, and after lying in a bottle six or eight months it made a beverage which some insisted ranked with dry champagne."[2] The large two-story building provided sufficient space for racking* and bottling the enormous quantity of cider produced on the Point and storing it until its sale. The Denning Cider Mill oversaw the whole process of growing, harvesting, and crushing the apples, as well as barreling and storing the resulting liquid until it fermented. Until at least 1872 all the cider produced came from apples grown on the Point, but the once-ample apple supply began to dwindle as builders removed the trees to make room for railroad

---

*Racking was the process of storing barrels on their sides and periodically turning them to encourage even fermentation.

Denning Cider Mill ruins looking east. Courtesy of the Beacon Historical Society.

tracks and brickyard buildings. In the mid-1870s mainland farmers began bringing their apples to the mill for processing. The proud tradition of using only apples grown on the Point for its famous cider slid into history as industrial incursion onto the Point gained momentum.

How did the Dennings transport hundreds of barrels of cider off the Point? Unfortunately, history proves silent as to the exact methods of transporting the cider, but boat and horse-drawn wagons seem likely, as does the railroad that ran along the very edge of the property.

The cider mill was saved from demolition by the narrowest of margins—probably less than three feet—when the Boston, Hartford, and Erie Railroad Company (the BH & E) began construction of a spur line to the end of the Point along its eastern shore. The cider mill was wedged between the roadbed and the water of Fishkill Bay. The railroad company began construction on the Point almost immediately after purchasing parts of it from the Denning women. The company's plan was an elaborate one. An official of the BH & E, quoted in the *Poughkeepsie Eagle* of June 10, 1869, remarked:

Southern Dutchess County as drawn on The Hudson by Daylight Map. *This map was drawn and published by William F. Link in 1878 as part of a Day Line Steamers brochure advertising journeys up the Hudson. Notice that the map's depiction of Denning's Point (bottom left corner) shows the road to the Dennings' mansion, but no evidence of railroad lines on the Point. Map references to historic places such as Washington's Headquarters, Hendrick Hudson's anchorage in Newburgh Bay, and the place where "a race of savages" once lived underline the commercial nature of the document. Courtesy of the Dutchess County Historical Society.*

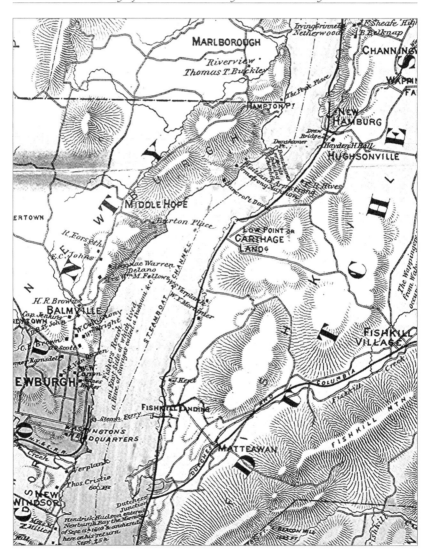

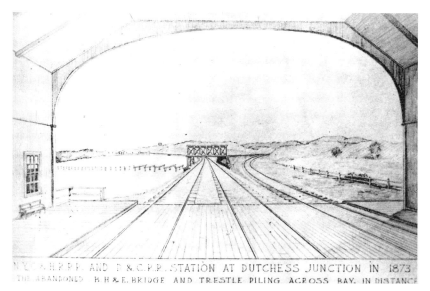

NYC&HRRR AND D&CRR STATION AT DUTCHESS JUNCTION IN 1873
THE ABANDONED BH&E BRIDGE AND TRESTLE PILING ACROSS BAY IN DISTANCE

The railroad station in Dutchess Junction in 1873 looking north toward Beacon with Denning's Point in the distance on the left. Notice the trestle over the tracks in the center of the picture and the pilings leading to Denning's Point. Collection of the Hudson Northern Model Train Club of Hopewell Junction, New York.

We commenced at Denning's Point, the western terminus of the road. There will be a trestle bridge from the crossing of the Hudson River Railroad to the extreme western end of Denning's Point, 3,000 feet in length. ... A locomotive house is already erected there and other necessary improvements have been made. Denning's Point will and should be an important place in the future as the Boston, Hartford and Erie Company will erect upon it machine shops and elegant buildings and docks will be constructed for the loading of boats from the Newburgh shore and along the river.[3]

The larger vision of the directors of the BH & E was an extremely ambitious one. Their plans included connecting southern New England to the mainline tracks to New York City as well as to the shipping port and ferry on the Hudson River at Denning's Point.

"Tracks were to be built from Connecticut through the southern part of Dutchess County to connect with the D & C/ND & C [Dutchess and Columbia / Newburgh, Dutchess, and Connecticut Railroad Company] at Hopewell. Hopewell was not yet a junction. Grading of this line was well under way but track laying at Hopewell had just begun when the failure came."[4]

In the few years during which they were solvent, the BH & E owners ordered construction of both a trestle bridge at Dutchess Junction and a major docking facility on the tip of Denning's Point. They laid track bed along the entire eastern shore of Denning's Point to connect it to the mainland. Workers built a trestle bridge across the Hudson River Railroad tracks near Fishkill Junction and drove pilings into Fishkill Bay on a curved line to intersect with the end of Denning's Point. The construction engineers designed the dock to receive railroad barges from across the river. No track was ever laid across the bay, but the pilings are still noted on official United States Government survey maps and can be seen in the illustration. All traces of the actual pilings are now either gone or below water level. Anyone walking along the eastern shore of the Point will notice a raised, straight path that was to have been the bed for the railroad. The natural contours of the eastern shore were altered forever.

One can only imagine the thoughts of the Denning women as they saw and heard the construction occurring all around their once-peaceful homestead. Physical aspects of the Point deteriorated as a result of the railroad incursion, and so did the Denning family fortune. Supreme Court papers issued from the Dutchess County Courthouse on September 2, 1870, reveal how closely the Denning's finances were tied to the plans of the railroad company owners and how precariously the Dennings were situated. The prologue of the document tells the story:

Emily Van Rensselaer & Jane L. Denning against The Boston Hartford and Erie Ferry Extension Rail Road Company,

The Boston Hartford and Erie Rail Road Company, James W. Taylor & George Townsend. — To the above named Defendants: Please to take Notice That the Summons herewith served upon you in this action is issued upon a complaint praying the foreclosure of a mortgage executed by The Boston Hartford & Erie Railroad Company to Emily Van Rensselaer & Jane L. Denning on the 15th day of November 1867 recorded in the office of the clerk of the County of Dutchess in Book of Mortgages, No. 117 page 608 C on the 18th day of February 1868 at 11:15 am. Said Mortgage was executed to secure the payment of the sum of ninety thousand dollars with interest from July 1, 1867 following described premises:[5]

The document continued in precise legal terms describing the Denning's Point property on which the Denning women had held the mortgage. In essence, the women sold and then held the mortgage to a small portion of land near the isthmus and two strips of land for roadbed on both shores of the Point. The Denning family retained possession of the land around their mansion, the cider mill, and most of the southern central part of the Point. Because of the filing of the above-mentioned suit in 1868, it is clear that Emily and her sister Jane were aware that the mortgage they held was in serious peril long before the finances of the railroad actually crashed in 1870. It had been a huge risk, and the Denning family stood to lose a strategic portion of their estate property, to say nothing of unrealized interest payments.

An article in the December 3, 1870, *Fishkill Standard* described the portion of Denning's Point that was considered Boston, Hartford, and Erie Railroad Company property. It reads:

THE DENNING POINT PROPERTY. The *Poughkeepsie Eagle* says the commission appointed by Judge Barnard, on application of the Dutchess and Columbia Railroad Company to ascertain the value of the property of the Boston, Hartford and Erie Railroad at Denning's Point, made their report on Monday morning. The property consists of 4 and ½ acres on Denning's Point, about 30 acres under water, and the trestle work. The report fixes the value of the property at $70,000.[6]

The words that almost slip by unnoticed are "30 acres under water." This is extremely important. In the notes in Charles Caldwell's 1878 survey field book, he stated specifically that water still broke through between the Point and the mainland at high tide.[7] A majority of those thirty underwater acres were soon filled by the construction of the rail line and subsequent brickyard operations.

An 1878 engineering map recovered from Newburgh's Engineering Archives clearly shows the swamp and marshland where fill was added. Careful examination of this map puts a great deal of

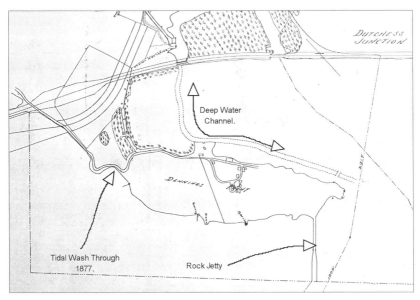

A section of a Caldwell map circa 1878 showing the marshlands between Denning's Point and the mainland. (Arrows added by the author for clarification.) Courtesy of the City of Newburgh Engineering Archives.

Denning's Point history into perspective. First, the map shows that Denning's Point was originally an island cut off from the mainland by marshland, especially during high tide. Second, it supports the first English name given to the Point, which was "the Island in Fishkill Bay," as well as Catherine Denning's renaming of it Presqu'ile, translated as "peninsula" or "almost an island," when the family added fill sufficient to support carriages.

Most importantly, the map distinctly shows the massive amount of fill necessary to bring the marshland between the island and mainland to levels capable of supporting large buildings and heavy industry. In 1881 Homer Ramsdell required huge quantities of fill to build the Denning's Point Brick Works. Additional quantities were necessary as late as 1925 during the rebuilding of the original 1881 Denning's Point Brickyard. A *Brick and Clay Record* article noted, "Construction problems were made more difficult by the plant being located over a virtual swamp. In some places it was necessary to make a fill of 14 feet to bring it up to the present levels."[8] That is an enormous amount of fill. The brickyard owners not only strip-mined the earth, they filled in waterways and marshlands with no consideration for the consequences of such actions on the environment. The Denning women found themselves caught in the middle of two rail lines, in addition to a massive ground-filling operation and new buildings that almost blocked their exit from the Point.

When the railroad company declared bankruptcy, records of the county failed to mention results of any court action indicating that the Denning women received financial remuneration. An article in the March 4, 1871, *Fishkill Standard* referred to the suit brought against the BH & E Railroad Company by Emily Van Rensselaer and Jane Denning, but noted the outlook was bleak for recovery as "it is believed the railroad company will ultimately take the property and finish their line of road."[9] After the bankruptcy, major shareholders received what was left before those who held mortgages on the property received any share. The BH & E failed in 1870 and took with it a strategic portion of Denning's Point.

Notice of the foreclosure auction ordered by the Supreme Court appeared a few years later, on April 27, 1872, in the *Fishkill Standard:*

VALUABLE PROPERTY AT AUCTION
At Newburgh, May 3d, 1872
By Order of the Supreme Court in Foreclosure
Will be sold at Public Auction, at the Orange Hotel,
In the city of Newburgh, on the third day of
May, 1872, at 12 o'clock, M.,
The Ferry Franchise and property known as the *Newburgh and Fishkill Ferry,* with its Ferryboats and Tackle,
and the land at the terminal at Fishkill and New-
Burgh, including the real estate at Newburgh, being
150 feet front on east side of Front Street, at the corner
of Second Street and the buildings thereon, and the
Steamboat Wharf.

Also a lot at the south-east corner of Front and
First streets, being 276 feet front on east side of
Front street and the lands under water adjacent there to.
Also the lands in the town of Fishkill, known as
Denning's Point and the Newline, Coleman, Wiltsie and
other properties, and lands under water adjacent there-
to, heretofore consigned to the Boston, Hartford and
Erie Ferry Extension Railroad Company.
Newburgh, N.Y., April 15th, 1872
E.A. Brewster, Referee.[10]

The article cited above was a bit misleading, for only part of Denning's Point was in fact lost in the failure of the BH & E. The mansion and its immediate environs, including the cider mill, remained in the hands of Emily and Jane Denning until 1889. Nevertheless, the sale included portions of the Point that complete-ly surrounded the estate, and the Dennings were not able to reacquire ownership of that land. The value, as well as the acreage, of the Denning estate ebbed away as industry slowly but surely moved in from all sides.

The subsequent newspaper report of the results of the auction briefly stated:

> The Supreme Court foreclosure sale of the ferry property, franchise, boats, and real estate, and the Denning Point, Newlin, Coleman, Wiltsie and other properties situated on this side of the river, known as the Boston, Hartford and Erie Ferry Extension Company estate, took place at Newburgh on Friday, 3d inst. Homer Ramsdell was the buyer at $125,000.[11]

Wealthy Homer Ramsdell played a large part in the evolving history of the Point. A court decree of March 1872 set the value of the property purchased by Ramsdell at $1 million. By paying merely $125,000, Ramsdell did extremely well. In light of the property loss by the popular Denning family and the undeniable gain by Ramsdell, it is clear why Homer Ramsdell might have been disliked and yet respected as a shrewd businessman. While Ramsdell did not then possess the mansion or its immediate grounds, he did own all of the surrounding property and exerted great influence on the local railroads.

Ramsdell was a controversial figure throughout the wider business community, as is reflected in this scathing description of him from a book entitled *The Old Merchants of New York City:*

> He was a little brainless counter-jumper at a small dry goods store, and used to get his six-penny dinners at Seely Brown's eating-house, No 51 Nassau street. ... He lacked everything but the impudence of Satan. He was pious in order to prosper; taught in the Sunday school of the Rev. Dr. Potts in order to have a good shye [try] at girls of fortune. This Ramsdell combed his hair beautifully. He was dressed to kill, but a man would have been deemed the veriest maniac out-

side of a lunatic asylum, had he whispered that the nice young man in the goods store in Maiden Lane—so harmless, so pleasant and kitten-like in his way of acting—so soft did he speak, and say, "Miss, what shall I show you today?"—that that half simpleton would be at the head of a mighty corporation and wield property worth tens of millions! Merchants, listen! Bankers of Wall Street, hearken! This poor devil in intellect, in experience—who could just count two and two makes four, could fix a silly girl—he was good looking, he was pious, and he cast his eyes around to make a match for money. He found a partner in Miss Powell of Newburgh, a daughter of the rich Thomas Powell who placed the son-in-law Homer Ramsdell, ex-dry-goods clerk, as President of the Erie railroad and its vast interests! Great heavens! Is it a wonder that under such a trifling chap that superb road should have gone to ruin, and carried with it thousands and tens of thousands of innocent people?[12]

The shrewdness of Ramsdell's choice of a spouse is undeniable. His wife's father, Thomas Powell, was not only a railroad magnate, but an influential and powerful man in the steamboat industry as well. Mr. Powell willed all of his steamboat and ferry holdings to his daughter, Mrs. Homer Ramsdell.

It was generally known, as testified by the citation above, that Homer Ramsdell had driven the Erie Railroad Company into near bankruptcy. In addition, the wily Ramsdell had connived to get himself elected to the board of directors of the Boston, Hartford & Erie Railroad Company in September of 1870 shortly before it finally did go bankrupt. He had thus placed himself in the position of knowing well in advance of the general public that the railroad was going to fold. Ramsdell also knew the enormous value of the property the railroad held, especially since it abutted the ferry property willed to his wife by her father. With the bankruptcy of the BH & E in 1870, the building of a shipping port and ferry dock on the South Rocks and the construction of the track bed along the eastern shore of the Point came to a halt. For the next ten years the remaining Denning family members—Jane, Emily, and her daughter Emily—lived in relative peace and quiet on the Point.

In the early 1880s the New York and New England Railroad Company (NY & NE)—the successor to the Boston, Hartford, and Erie Railroad Company—bought the last vestiges of Denning property remaining on the Point, claiming it was necessary for their plans. One should not be surprised to learn that Homer Ramsdell was also on the board of the NY & NE. The Dennings were most likely forced to sell their remaining property under the guidelines of eminent domain. This was carefully orchestrated by Homer Ramsdell, who benefited enormously. "After making a deep cut through the Point, almost severing it, and destroying a number of trees, the company decided on a new route for their road and sold the place, subject to a life estate to Miss Denning."[13] The person to whom the NY & NE sold Denning's Point was none other than the scheming Homer Ramsdell. This purchase gave him complete control over the use of Denning's Point. The Dennings were unable to raise the money necessary to buy back the land, so it ultimately all ended up in the hands of Homer Ramsdell. The Dennings were permitted to stay as long as they liked—or more likely, until they could no longer live amidst the railroad and industrial din and dirt.

The pastoral beauty of Denning's Point was quickly extinguished as progress, in the form of railroad and industry, slowly moved forward. When Jane Denning died in March 1889, the remaining two Denning women—Mrs. Emily Denning Van Rensselaer and her daughter, Miss Emily Denning Van Rensselaer—left the Point and moved into town. In a postscript to the *Recollections of Presqu'ile* by Mrs. Emily Denning Van Rensselaer, an unnamed cousin closes out the story of life on the Point:

> The house, which had hardly contained the large family of which she [Mrs. Emily Denning Van Rensselaer] speaks, was

now far too large and burdensome a care in her advanced
years. Brickyards had begun to cut into the upper end of the
Point, and the railroad had crossed the lower part, cutting a
great scar in the green lawn and converting the South Rocks
into a starting point for a dock which extended far into the
river. All privacy was gone, and this lovely spot was completely destroyed as a dwelling place. So with deep sorrow, felt by
every member of the family and also by those who had at any
time enjoyed the hospitality of that charming place, the
furniture was packed up, and a new home was started a few
miles away more suitable in size to the diminished household but which is still presided over by the same sweet presence, and the same warm welcome is always in readiness for
those who are so fortunate as to enjoy the hospitality, still
continued here, which was begun so many years ago.[14]

*Rear foundation wall of the Denning Mansion ruins facing south. Notice the
rectangular, flat, finished stonework, which defines this as the rear of the building.
Photograph by Jim Heron.*

The whole community felt the loss. In August 1889 the *Fishkill Standard* noted the event with grief:

> Denning's Point, which has been for so many years a delightful place of residence by the Denning family, is about to be given up by those who now reside there. Mrs. Van Rensselaer is the last of the Denning family at the Point, the others having all passed away. The family will move this fall, we understand, and occupy the Campbell place, near Mr. Burnham's.[15]

The fame of the mansion was such that even The *New York Times* noted, on January 3, 1890, that the Point was no longer in the hands of the Denning family.[16]

The story of the Denning family did not end with their move from the Point; mother and daughter continued to make their marks on the nearby community. Though they had lost much financially, they remained ladies of considerable means. They continued the practice of giving and sharing that had marked the earlier years of the Denning family and that knit the Denning name forever into the very fabric of the Fishkill Landing community. Mrs. Emily Denning Van Rensselaer died in 1898, but her daughter Emily continued the good works until her own death. Her many acts of charity included donating money to build the first black church in Beacon. She financed the building of the Women's Christian Temperance Union building in Fishkill Landing, and fortunately left this mortal sphere before it was turned into a liquor store. Miss Emily Denning Van Rensselaer gave so generously, and sometimes so foolishly, that she, the last of the Dennings from Denning's Point, died in abject poverty in 1931.

While it was a disaster for the Denning family, the failure of the Boston, Hartford and Erie Railroad Company probably saved the Point itself from being entirely consumed by railroad and industrial interests. At the time of the BH & E failure, plans for industrialization

Northwest corner of the Denning Mansion ruins. Notice the roughly cut rock foundations and compare with the rear wall's smoothly cut stone. Photograph by Jim Heron.

of the Point included a port and a major ferry crossing at the very tip of the Point. By the time the line was reorganized under the name of the New York and New England Railroad Company, the ferry docks at Fishkill Landing, about one mile north of Denning's Point, were in operation. Therefore, plans to build a port and ferry dock on Denning's Point itself were dropped. Homer Ramsdell owned the port and ferry dock at Fishkill Landing, and profited tremendously because it was then virtually impossible to cross the Hudson River in the vicinity of Beacon without going through Ramsdell's property and paying to use his ferries. If the BH & E had not failed, Denning's Point would probably have become a busy dock and ferry station surrounded by associated buildings and track lines. As history played out, the Point was bypassed for railroad development, but Homer Ramsdell had other plans to exploit the land for his own financial gain.

CHAPTER 6

THE EARLY YEARS OF THE
DENNING'S POINT
BRICK WORKS

1880–1920

WITH THOUGHTS OF HOMER RAMSDELL'S BUSINESS PRACTICES FRESH IN MY MIND, I FOUND MY NEXT EXCURSION TO THE POINT WAS WITH A SPIRIT FAR LESS BUOYANT THAN IN MY EARLIER WALKS. THE EVOLVING STORY OF ITS PAST WAS NOW TINGED WITH GREED. THE HISTORY WAS ABOUT TO ENTER AN ERA OF INDUSTRIALIZATION, ROBBER BARONS, BIG-DOLLAR DEALS, AND FACTORIES. THE EARLY INDUSTRY OPERATED WITHOUT REGARD FOR THE LAND AND ITS RESOURCES, WHILE SUBSEQUENT INDUSTRY NEITHER ADDED TO NOR DIMINISHED THE ALREADY RAVISHED LAND. DENNING'S POINT WAS IN FOR A MAJOR SHOCK, A PROCESS KNOWN IN THE BUSINESS WORLD AS "PROGRESS," AND IT WAS THE ACTIONS OF HOMER RAMSDELL THAT BEGAN THE PROCESS THAT CHANGED FOREVER THE FACE OF THE POINT AND THE ADJOINING MAINLAND.

Homer Ramsdell, by virtue of his 1872 purchase of most of the Point and all of the adjoining Wiltsie and Newlin properties, was the primary player in the early brickyard years. From the onset of his tenure, even before he began to build the brickyard, Ramsdell assumed an extremely possessive stance regarding his purchase on the riverfront. By 1876 Ramsdell had fenced off the entrance to the Point and took great umbrage at anybody who dared trespass on this as yet undeveloped land. Although the Denning family still resided on the most western portions of the Point and had free access to their home, Ramsdell owned the entrance and guarded it jealously.

Ramsdell's attempts to control access were noted in the following citation from the September 22, 1877, *Fishkill Standard*:

> Trespassing upon Denning's Point, especially upon Sundays, by parties who engage in clam bakes, boat racing, and carousing generally, has become such a nuisance to the residents on the Point, that Mr. Homer Ramsdell gives notice thorough our columns, this week, forbidding all visitors on Sundays, and only by permission on week days. As there is a heavy penalty for trespassing, persons who propose to visit the Point unlawfully, should change their intentions before they get themselves into serious trouble.[1]

History proves that Ramsdell's threat was no deterrent, however. The people of Fishkill Landing, Matteawan, and Byrnesville considered the Point theirs to use for recreational purposes. Tales of their

Brick from Denning's Point Brick Works. Photograph by Jim Heron.

enjoyment unfold alongside the stories of burgeoning industry on the Point. Lost was the sense of awe in which the Point was held during the glory years of the Denning family. Lost was the time when trespassing on Denning's land was prohibited by social convention because of the esteem in which the Denning family was held by the community. There was no need of signs then, nor need of newspaper warnings; local villagers courteously asked the family, and it appears that they were always granted permission to use the shores of the Point. Concurrently with the advent of the railroad and the beginning of the brickworks, however, a communal sense of possession regarding the Point seems to have developed among the local people similar to the attitude of the Native Americans who had first lived on this same parcel of land.

In 1880, with legal control over property on and around the Point, Homer Ramsdell had ample land to begin the building of a huge brickyard. Brick making was already a thriving business in the area, since both banks of the Hudson contained rich clay deposits. Homer Ramsdell plotted the details of a business endeavor that

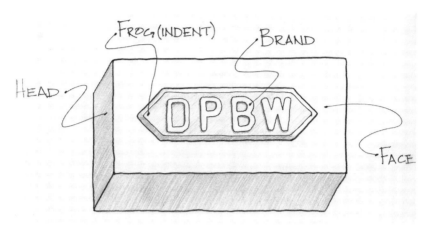

The Anatomy of a Brick. Sketch by Timothy David Heron.

would add to his wealth as it stripped the land of its natural resources. An article in the August 11, 1880, edition of the *Poughkeepsie Eagle* detailed his construction plans:

> Another Brickyard in Fishkill—The Newburgh Journal says Homer Ramsdell, of that city, is about to build a large brick-yard on the east side of Denning's Point—at the north end of the cove, and north of the channel formed by the outlet of Fishkill Creek, by which channel access may be had to the river for vessels drawing as much as ten feet of water. ... It is to be furnished with a powerful steam engine and the most improved machinery and will be calculated to turn out from eight to ten millions of brick a season, but it is to be so con-structed that it will form a part of a series of brickyards a thousand feet in length with a capacity of fifty millions of brick per year, should the demand warrant this production.[2]

The article raved about the high quality of the clay expected on the Denning's Point property as well as on the adjacent property, and predicted sufficient clay to last for several centuries. "In all respects,

Top, the main manufacturing building looking north. The dock to the left of the building has a barge awaiting loading. The long narrow buildings to the right of the larger building are drying sheds. Bottom, one of the Denning's Point clay banks. Three men appear as white specks on the top of the over fifty-feet-high clay bank. Photograph courtesy of the Tamiment Library and Robert F. Wagner Labor Archives, New York University.

for accessibility and convenience of management, it is claimed that the yard will be the equal of any on the North River."[3] *

By late in 1880, the building of the brickyard was well underway under the direction of Alexander McLean. McLean oversaw the leveling of portions of the existing Denning's Point, Wiltsie, and Newlin properties and brought in an enormous amount of fill to deepen and widen the neck of the peninsula near the mainland. The land had to be level in order to erect kilns, mixing vats, drying yards, and necessary buildings. The October 23, 1880, issue of the *Fishkill Standard* gave a complaisant description of this process that affected the prime and beautiful landscape: "The deposit of clay is covered with

---

*The Hudson River was known as the North River, and the Delaware River as the South River, until well into the nineteenth century.

a light upper crust of earth and many trees, but these are easily removed and beneath them is an inexhaustible deposit of clay."[14] Thus, the land was altered dramatically even before Ramsdell's brickyard workers began to mine the valuable clay.

By March 1881 the site boasted two sheds, each containing the necessary machinery for two clay pits. "Besides these two sheds, there have been erected an engine house and a blacksmith shop, while a boarding house for employees is now being built. It will be 'T' shaped, and measure 20 feet by 36 feet one way, and 16 feet by 36 feet the other. It will contain two stories and a cellar. Besides the boarding-house, two smaller houses for the men to sleep in will be built."[5]

While building the boardinghouse on the Point, workers discovered what the April 2, 1881, *Fishkill Standard* identified as "relics."[6] According to the newspaper, the workers found a loose cornerstone with the date 1738 carved into its face, a 1706 British halfpenny coin, and an American halfpenny coin dated 1726. The date on the stone immediately intrigued me. I wondered if this stone marked Jacobus de

Hauling clay in the early 1900s. Photograph courtesy of CH Energy Group, Inc.

The DPBW blacksmith shop with narrow-gauge brickyard railroad cars piled with clay. Photograph courtesy of CH Energy Group, Inc.

Peyster's ownership of the Point (which he purchased in 1738), or whether it was the actual cornerstone of his home. As the owner of the Point and all that was on it from 1738 to 1789, the estate of Jacobus de Peyster was the landlord from whom Alexander Hamilton rented a dwelling place in 1781. If the boardinghouse associated with the brickworks was built on the same location as the de Peyster house rented by Hamilton, then the foundations of the Hamilton rental and the place in which he penned documents important to the history of the United States have been lost. Because the builders of the boardinghouse found the dated stone unattached to any other foundation building material, however, it is quite possible that the stone had been carried by collectors, scavengers, or looters from a location farther out on the Point and simply left at the site of the later construction. If that were the case, then the exact location of the Hamilton rental remains unidentified. Unless archeologically sound evidence of de Peyster's foundation is found elsewhere on the Point, the cornerstone will remain a part of the intriguing puzzle of early American life on the Point.

In addition to equipment sheds and a boardinghouse for employees, the brickworks required shipping facilities for its finished product. McLean oversaw the construction of a 600-foot dock that spanned the entire head of the cove; the docking area was on land newly created by the addition of fill, and not on a part of the original Denning's Point. By this time in the construction process, the natural configuration of Denning's Point had been permanently changed by the addition of so much fill that most of the original eastern shore of Denning's Point was completely obscured. Shipping operations called for the docking of brick barges drawing as much as ten feet of water regardless of tide. Thus, in addition to changing the configuration of the land, workers also used a dredging machine to deepen the channel in Fishkill Bay to fifteen feet. The *Fishkill Standard* of June 7, 1890, noted: "E.M. Payn & Co., of Albany, are doing some work for Homer Ramsdell in dredging out the channel at Denning's Point."[7]

The combination of construction dirt and general busyness in the area, combined with Ramsdell's stubborn determination to keep the locals off his property, limited local access by land to the Point for recreational purposes. The Point still remained a popular location for fishing and bathing, however; area residents adapted their method of entry and accessed their favorite sites by water, either from the river side of the Point or from the bay side.

The various aspects of brickyard construction continued at a frantic pace. By April 1881 manufacturing operations commenced. The brick industry in the area provided jobs for local people; the brickyard on Denning's Point employed up to 150 men for most of its operating days. In the 1880s the brick industry paid wages that varied between $1.50 and $2.00 per day for skilled labor, and between $1.00 and $1.40 per day for unskilled workers. "The workday varied between ten hours and fourteen hours, with the average at twelve hours."[8] The economic importance of the brickyards along the Hudson River was underscored by the printing of daily brick prices on the front page of many newspapers in brickyard communities.

The mudroom where bricks were formed before being fired. Photograph courtesy of the Beacon Historical Society

It was the land itself, however, that paid the real price as Homer Ramsdell's brickyard consumed the natural resources. An April 30, 1881, article in the *Fishkill Standard* noted: "Instead of its former wild and deserted character, it has become the scene of busy industry and a great transformation has already been wrought, and is still being made. Where there were trees and unsightly shrubbery, there are now buildings either up or being erected; a level plain made; and men and horses are active in working still further change."[9] The pristine land and adjacent waters were deemed of less value than economic progress, and their preservation was totally disregarded as the Denning's Point Brick Works (DPBW) flourished. Champions for the environment were rare in the 1800s.

The first bricks that emerged from the DPBW on April 26, 1881, were greeted with great celebration. The site Ramsdell chose for brick production was perfect, and those who predicted rich clay deposits proved to be correct. Charles Ellery Hall, in his authoritative 1905 book *The Story of Bricks*, noted that the clay deposits on Denning's Point ran from twenty-five feet to seventy-five feet in depth. Hall also mentioned that the river afforded an abundance of quicksand, which produced higher-quality bricks than the common sand used in most brick making. "Clay is already being dredged from the river bed to supplement the product of the higher level. It is proposed also to make the works eat up the greater part of Denning's Point itself."[10] Thus, because the Point was favored at the time of its creation with convenient location and desirable natural resources, it was targeted for exploitation.

Brick making was a seasonal industry and operated only during the warmer months of the year to keep kiln-heating expenses within reason. Production was maximized during those months in order to keep the building industry supplied with brick during the months the brickyards stood idle. Production in the early years was modest according to Hudson Valley standards; the two initial DPBW machines turned out 66,000 bricks a day.[11] Site expansion continued, however, while the brickyard produced this steady flow of bricks, many marked with DPBW to identify it as a product of the Denning's Point Brick Works. Within twenty years—by around the year 1900—the trustees of the Estate of Homer Ramsdell then managing the brickyard increased the number of brick-making machines to seven and boasted a daily output of 154,000 bricks. Striving for even greater output, the brickyard management laid plans in 1905 for eleven more machines and began the inevitable change from steam-driven machines and shovels to more efficient, electrically powered brick-making machines.[12]

The brickworks initially strip-mined enough clay and sand from the Point or from the adjacent property on the west side of the rail line to keep the machines supplied with raw materials. Early documentation of the mining locations failed to distinguish between clay and sand deposits. Recent discoveries (see Chapter 9) reveal that much of the sand that was used was mined from the shore of the river just off the northwestern side of the Point. This explains the precipitous drop-off along that side of the Point and the subsequent significant erosion along that entire shoreline. With the increased production, however, even this massive and invasive mining failed to produce sufficient sand for the brick-making machines. In order to augment their supply, the DPBW bought a share of the Plum Point Sand Bank Company of New Windsor, which owned a rich sand-mining area on the west side of the Hudson River.

During the first fourteen years of operation, Homer Ramsdell, as the owner of the brickworks, was singled out as the target for numerous malicious and destructive acts perpetrated by people on both sides of the river. The *New York Times* recorded the burglary of the Ramsdell home, as well as many cases of arson on Ramsdell properties. These properties were not insured, so the owner had to assume the full loss.[13]

The actions against the DPBW indicated the high level of local animosity personally directed toward Ramsdell. The *Newburgh Journal* of May 12, 1891, recorded one of the attempts to wreck the DPBW:

Denning's Point circa 1900. Notice the horseshoe-shaped excavation on the Point in the right center. The DPBW consumed the Point as work progressed southward. Photograph courtesy of the Tamiment Library and Robert F. Wagner Labor Archives, New York University.

Yesterday morning the breaking of a piece of machinery in a brickyard led to the revelation of a deliberate plot to wreck that yard. Had the scheme been consummated the yard would have been damaged to the extent of thousands of dollars, all operations would have been stopped, and the lives of thirty men endangered. The Denning's Point Brick Company—which is virtually composed of the Messrs. Ramsdell, of Newburgh—was apparently singled out by the fiend, or fiends, for the purpose of this dastardly attempt.[14]

The article explained in great detail how stones and pieces of iron were placed precisely in the parts of the machines where they would do the most damage and yet not be seen until the machine began operations. The article noted that if the machines had been started, disaster would have been assured:

Had the plan been carried out the machinery would have broken with a crash and the pieces would have been sent flying in all directions, probably killing some of the men who were at work in the vicinity and injuring others. But fortunately the scheme failed. There were five machines started when the day's work began. All went well, until suddenly there was a crash in one of the machines. A piece of metal was broken from its place, being thrown against the breast of a man felling him instantly to the ground. A cylinder in another machine was broken before the steam was shut off.[15]

Major damage was averted by the quick actions of those manning the machines. This sabotage plan required significant knowledge of brick-making machines, implying that it was accomplished by insiders. It is interesting to note that of all the brickyards in the area, only the DPBW was targeted for this kind of deliberate destruction. It is quite clear that Homer Ramsdell made numerous local enemies. As further evidence of local animosity toward Homer Ramsdell, his death in 1894 brought an abrupt end to both the arson attempts on his Newburgh properties and the sabotage of the DPBW.

The *New York Times* obituary for Homer Ramsdell detailed his accomplishments and provided a long list of his holdings, but reported nothing about his personal character. "He was interested in almost every considerable undertaking of his time in that locality [Newburgh], and was the originator of many projects that have proved of great benefit to that city. He was a large stockholder in factories, railroads, banks, steamboats, docks, and storehouses."[16] The *Newburgh Journal,* in its four-column full-page obituary, also noted Ramsdell's extraordinary holdings in dozens of different enterprises, but failed to ascribe any personal attributes and omitted mention of the Denning's Point Brick Works. How could this comprehensive obituary completely fail to speak of his business on Denning's Point? Possibly Denning's Point was such a small part of his vast empire of holdings that it was unworthy of remark. Or perhaps the pointed comment in the *Newburgh Journal* that "in some quarters he was not appreciated"[17] was all that needed to be said about Ramsdell's endeavors on Denning's Point.

The subsequent account in the *Newburgh Journal* of Homer Ramsdell's funeral mentioned attendance by all the industrial tycoons of the time from the Newburgh area, but left out any mention of his accomplishments. The same newspaper article commented that six Episcopal clergymen officiated and that Ramsdell's family walked behind the coffin, but it failed to give any of their names, while each of the many dignitaries was individually identified.[18] Apparently both respected and detested, Homer Ramsdell remains a colorful part of the history of Denning's Point.

After his death and until the closing of the brickyard, the trustees of the Estate of Homer Ramsdell managed the property. No doubt the townspeople welcomed the complete turnabout in attitude exhibited by the trustees regarding recreational use of the properties. By the end of the 1800s, the trustees facilitated local passage to the Point's recreational areas alongside, and sometimes even through, the center of the massive brickworks. The number of people eager to enjoy leisure-time opportunities on the Point burgeoned as the local population swelled dramatically during the construction and early years of operation of the brickworks. The Federal Census data of 1800, 1850, and 1880 shows a regular and rapid increase in population of the areas immediately adjacent to the Point.* After 1880 and through 1920, Denning's Point saw steadily increasing recreational use by the local population. The August 11, 1900, *Fishkill Standard* claimed:

> So popular has the Denning's Point become as a picnic spot, that it has been denominated as Fishkill's Coney Island. It bears about the same relation to the two villages as does Coney Island to the Greater New York. Every day families, individuals, and parties go there and enjoy the cooling breezes, the bathing in waters of the Hudson, and the good things they take along to eat and enjoy in picnic fashion.[19]

In scenes that are unlikely to be enacted on private property in today's litigious society, old photographs exhibit images of crowds of people reveling on the Point. Fun was accompanied by a few bothersome hazards, however. An article published in July 1900 warned picnickers to take precautions:

---

*The Federal Census of 1800 showed a population of 5,678 in the town of Fishkill, which included East Fishkill, Lagrange, Wappingers Falls, Fishkill Landing, Matteawan, and part of Phillipstown. The 1880 Federal Census carefully delineated towns and villages and thus included much less territory. This census showed Fishkill Landing with a population of 2,517, Matteawan with a population of 4,411 and the village of Byrnesville with a population of 213. Thus, the total 1880 population surpassed that of the entire town of Fishkill's 1800 population, and was more than half again the area's numeration in 1850.

The jetty, taken from the west coast of the Point looking out toward the Hudson River. Photograph courtesy of the Southern Dutchess Chamber of Commerce.

1915 version of the Sports Illustrated *swimsuit issue. Photograph courtesy of the Beacon Historical Society.*

"Courting on the Point," dated 1900. Photograph courtesy of the Beacon Historical Society.

"Newburgh Dock Rats," sponsored by the Newburgh Canoe and Boating Association, during their 1904 encampment on Denning's Point close to the shoreline on the bay side. Left, Denning Mansion. Photograph courtesy of the Newburgh Heritage Center.

Picnic on Denning's Point, dated June 4, 1911, by the tape on the bottom left corner of the picture. Photograph courtesy of the Beacon Historical Society.

The Perils of Picnicking at Denning's Point: Picnicking at Denning's Point has its troubles as well as its pleasures. It is a free ground for everybody. There is no police force. The good and the bad have equal access to it. The hoodlum element is largely represented, and they make life anything but pleasant for picnic parties not provided with ample male protection.[20]

The *Beacon News* article continued by detailing the story of the "hoodlum element" stealing the lunches of unescorted young ladies as the ladies sailed in the bay, and recounting that the hoodlums threw a bottle of olive oil at the chaperone as she tried to recover the picnic. The miscreants were caught and the newspaper suggested: "They should be arrested and given a lesson that will teach them to be honest, instead of indulging in petty thieving. If they will steal small things now, they will steal larger things as they grow older, and become hardened criminals."[21]

A great variety of recreational activities were popular on Denning's Point during this time period. The *Newburgh Journal* recorded a wonderful event that took place in late June through early July 1915 when Denning's Point served as the location of the annual meet and camp of the Atlantic division of the American Canoe Association. This was a major affair that lasted a full week, with at least 500 canoe enthusiasts camping on the Point while competing in different categories of canoe races on the Hudson River. Hundreds of spectators came to watch the races and participate in the fun. The many news articles about the event implied that socializing among the competitors and having a thoroughly enjoyable time were as important as the outcomes of the races. Events included handicapping heats, cruising races, canoe-filling competitions, and exhibitions of canoe handling. The canoe-tilting matches were extremely popular. While two canoeists paddled the canoe into position, a third canoeist balanced himself on the gunwales of the canoe with a long, padded pole in hand. A second canoe, similarly manned, maneuvered into position, with the object being to knock the competing balanced canoeist into the water. The canoe-filling contest was equally hilarious. Two or three people in each of two canoes tried to capsize or sink others by hurling pails full of water at them.

One eye-catching sub-headline from the collection of articles describing the Canoe Association's festivities was entitled "How Squaws Spent Spare Time."[22] The reference to "squaws" did not, as one might be led to believe, indicate that Native American women participated in the event. Rather, it was a dismissive term applied in general to the female campers. The newspaper article in the June 29, 1915, *Newburgh Journal* said it all:

Yesterday was a very quiet day in camp. Most of the men went to Poughkeepsie, leaving the Point early in the morning and going up the river in their big war canoes.... This left Vice Commodore F. Edward Ahrens remaining in charge

Getting ready for a race off Denning's Point at the 1915 American Canoe Association's meeting. Photograph courtesy of the Southern Dutchess Chamber of Commerce.

Same event as above, but this picture was taken from the top of the hill at the very end of Denning's Point. Photograph courtesy of the Southern Dutchess Chamber of Commerce.

and the "squaws" keeping engaged in preparing food against the return of the braves. The "squaw camp" was a busy camp in the afternoon, despite the absence of the men. Some of the women had their embroidery work to occupy their attention. Others were engaged in the more homely but also more necessary duties of the housewife, such as peeling potatoes, preparing other vegetables for the evening meal and the other work needed just as much about the camp as about home.[23]

A caption from a picture entitled "Caring for the Inner Man at Canoeists' Camp" continued to paint a demeaning picture of women's roles. The caption read: "The picture was caught by a staff photographer of *The News* as Mrs. Baldwin and Mrs. Clark of the Inwood 'squaws' were preparing the 'chuck' against the return of the 'starving braves.' "[24]

A more independent spirit did show in several of the women in camp, however. "Perhaps the most fun was enjoyed by Miss Grace E. Marshall, Miss Clara Friede and Miss Eugenia Wallach. Clad in their bathing dresses—the derigor [sic] costume for the beach—these three young women commandeered a canoe belonging to one of the men. With this craft they explored the east shore of the Hudson from Bannerman's Island to the ferry slip. Not the least of their enjoyment came from the frequent dips overboard."[25]

A careful examination of these pictures reveals not only the canoeists participating in the event, but also up-to-date electric boats for sightseers. These boats often carried people from Newburgh to the Point to enjoy the beaches and participate in events like the canoe meeting.

The American Canoe Association meet ended on Sunday, July 4, with election of officers and a grand end-of-race party.[26] It must have been a very exciting gathering, made possible by the trustees of Homer Ramsdell's estate generously permitting recreational use of the land.

In addition to the picnicking, sun-bathing, wading, canoeing, swimming, and sailing on and around the Point, considerable recreational fishing took place there. A 1904 *Beacon News* article mentioned one such fishing party:

> Down by Denning's Point: George Harris, jr., of Matteawan, has a fine new net which he purchased last winter. He is fond of fish and fishing, and Thursday he invited a whole lot of his friends to go down to Denning's Point to try their luck. Harris has a lot of friends, or else Matteawan people are fond of the festive shad. At any rate Matteawan had the appearance of a deserted village for several hours on Thursday. A number of public officials were on hand and took in hauling in the seine. Some of the "boys" worked harder than they have for years past. Three hauls were made, and 15 noble shad were captured, besides an unlimited amount of herring and bass. The delicious odors of baked shad, fried shad, and planked shad were wafted on the breeze all that evening and tantalized the yearning stomach of those who are not of the faithful.[27]

The brickyard remained a competitive part of the brick-making industry in the Hudson Valley for the first two decades of 1900. The occasional strikes were short-lived and generally nonviolent. Whenever the supply of bricks in the valley exceeded the demand, the DPBW, like its competitors, closed for a period of months until prices returned to a profitable level. Manufacturing downtimes were few and far between, however, making the DPBW an asset to the economies of Fishkill Landing, Matteawan, and Byrnesville before 1913, and to the economy of the city of Beacon after all three villages incorporated together that year.

The 1920s saw the DPBW rise to the apex of the brick-manufacturing business in the Hudson Valley. David J. Strickland's arrival at the DPBW in 1925 marked the beginning of a revolution in the brick-making industry. His genius in brick-machine design and over-all brickyard organization brought Denning's Point production to new heights, and also put in motion the course of action whose consequence was the ultimate demise of the Denning's Point brick industry.

CHAPTER 7

THE PEAK AND COLLAPSE
OF THE BRICKWORKS

1920–1940

WHEN NEXT I WALKED THE PENINSULA, WITH THE DETAILS OF THE DENNING'S POINT BRICK WORKS FRESH IN MY MIND, I IMAGINED ENTERING INTO THE MIDST OF A FUNCTIONING BRICKYARD WITH ALL THE NOISE OF THE ENGINES, THE ROAR OF FIRE IN THE KILNS, THE RUMBLE OF THE MIXERS, AND THE JUMBLE OF THE MANY DIFFERENT LANGUAGES SPOKEN BY THE LABORERS. I IMAGINED HEARING PHRASES SHOUTED BY NATIVE SONS OF IRELAND, HUNGARY, GERMANY, ITALY, CZECHOSLOVAKIA, POLAND, AND GREECE. I ENVISIONED THE RUSH OF EXCITE-MENT OF BEING IMMERSED IN A VIBRANT MANUFACTURING ENVIRONMENT. I KNEW THAT THE BRICKWORKS HAD VIRTUALLY WRECKED THE POINT, YET FOR THE FIRST TIME I COMPREHENDED, AT LEAST IN PART, HOW EASILY THE EXHIL-ARATION AND SEDUCTION OF MASSIVE PRODUCTION MIGHT CAUSE BLINDNESS TO THE WREAKING OF ENVIRONMENTAL HAVOC. I LOOKED FORWARD TO RESEARCH INTO THE LIVES OF THE PEOPLE—AND INTERVIEWING THOSE WHO ARE STILL ALIVE—WHOSE EXPERIENCES INCLUDED BRICK MAKING ON THE POINT.

The business of making bricks remained as fiercely competitive in 1920 as it was back in 1881 when Ramsdell's Denning's Point Brick Works (DPBW) produced its first brick. By 1920 every brick factory in the Hudson Valley strove to keep up with new methods and to install new machines in order to remain viable in this competitive business. Industrial espionage was commonplace; neither new methods nor novel machines were kept secret for very long. The area brickyards vied to feed New York City's enormous appetite for building material, driving intense competition and resulting in lowered scruples.

One common aspect of remaining competitive was keeping production costs low, including expenditures for workers. Labor conditions inside the DPBW in the 1920s were far from ideal. Brickyard workers labored nine and one-half hours on the day shift (7:00 am–4:30 pm) or eight and one-half hours on the night shift (4:30 pm–1:00 am)[1] They worked within an inherently dangerous environment. Machinery for brick making was heavy, powerful, and fast. It left little room for error. Loss of fingers and sometimes limbs was the price paid for even a moment's inattention to the ever-moving parts of the machines. Brick dust generated during brick making caused respiratory discomfort and sometimes long-term lung damage. The loading and mixing tasks involved hefting extremely heavy loads that, if dropped, could crush a man. Even workers whose only task was to excavate clay were at great risk. A 1923 story in the *Beacon Evening Journal* reported:

TONS OF CLAY IN LANDSLIDE AT BRICKYARD—Operator of Steam Shovel and Workers Escape as Machine is buried.

Three men, working near the steam shovel at the Denning's Point brickyard, narrowly escaped injury or possible death yesterday afternoon when, without warning, over two hundred tons of wet clay broke loose from its bank and slid down upon the shovel in a monstrous landslide.[2]

The article additionally detailed that avalanching clay moved the steam shovel twenty feet and smashed the operator's cab beyond recognition.

Despite the long hours and inherent risks, the workforce in 1925 was paid $3.75 to $4.50 for a full day, which was a modest wage even for the times.[3] By comparison, in 1914 Henry Ford was paying his workers $5.00 a day for an eight-hour shift.[4] Moreover, life within the yards was a world unto itself, and many considered the brickyards to be "the most lawless section of the county."[5] Even though the DPBW was regarded as one of the least dangerous yards, two murders were committed there, "on the job," in the twelve years between 1926[6] and 1937.[7] * The owners of the brickworks were committed to rapid production of quality building bricks to sell at competitive prices, and only tangentially attentive to labor relations and conditions.

The DPBW manufactured bricks at the rate of more than 150,000 per day in the early 1920s. During this time brickyard equipment was slowly upgraded from steam-driven to more modern, electrically driven machines, allowing Denning's Point to hold its own in competition with other area brickyards. It soon became evident to the owners of the brickworks, however, that merely holding one's own was insufficient to maintain a prominent place in this industry. The trustees of the Estate of Homer Ramsdell recognized that the brickyard needed changes in both leadership and direction, and began to search for a qualified person to spearhead these endeavors.

---

* Robert Griswold was murdered in 1926, and Thomas Fasula was murdered in 1937. Both assailants were caught and convicted.

Inside of the main building of the Denning's Point Brick Works in 1925 as it was being rebuilt under the supervision of David Strickland. Photograph courtesy of the Beacon Historical Society.

A side view of the 1925 rebuilding of the DPBW under the supervision of David Strickland. Photograph courtesy of the Beacon Historical Society.

One of the two new Strickland brick machines that manufactured 200,000 bricks per day. Photograph courtesy of Brick and Clay Journal.

In late 1925 the search ended with the hiring of David Strickland to reorganize and upgrade the DPBW. Strickland came to the Point with an impressive record that included building and designing brick plants, as well as inventing some of the most important machinery in the brick-making industry. He arrived holding twelve United States patents for brick machines, dumping apparatus, and handling devices, and added another four patents while building and managing the Denning's Point facility. Strickland created a fresh layout, using newly designed machines "which set it [the DPBW] aside or rather ahead of most other plants,"[8] instead of tinkering with previous plans or attempting to correct minor flaws in the Denning's Point operation. "A study of the plant reveals a total disregard of precedent in laying out the machinery and equipment for practically every process involved in transforming the raw clay in the pit to burned brick."[9] The genius of David Strickland put the DPBW at the top of the entire industry within five years.

Electric setting machine taking brick directly out of the wheeled car and unloading it into the kiln. Photograph courtesy of Brick and Clay Journal.

Electric shovel and narrow-gauge clay-hauling cars implemented by Strickland. Photograph courtesy of CH Energy Group, Inc.

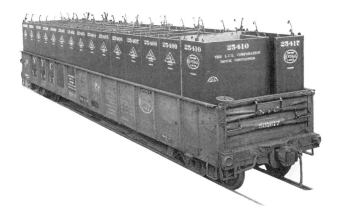

The patented Strickland brick railroad shipping container. Photograph courtesy of the Strickland family.

The revised plant design called for only two machines, both of them designed and built by Strickland. Before Strickland's renovations, the DPBW ran eleven or more machines. Those eleven machines, even in times of peak operation, failed to approach the efficiency of production or the volume yielded by the two new Strickland machines. Each of Strickland's machines produced 100,000 bricks per day per shift, which was an enormous number compared with competing brickyards. To push yield even higher, Strickland implemented a second shift on one of the machines to raise production to a total of 300,000 bricks a day. Subsequently he added a double shift on the second machine to increase the factory's daily output to 400,000 bricks. This was the first time in the history of the Hudson River brick industry that a plant worked double shifts to keep up with the demand for brick.[10] Double shifts of workers and the resulting prodigious output quickly made the DPBW the single largest producer of bricks in the entire Hudson Valley.

Several significant features specific to Strickland's plant design are noteworthy. He constructed two railroad spurs running directly into the middle of the brickyard's drying shed, a detail noted on the

Strickland brick containers being unloaded. Photograph by Pawling and Harnischfeger Corporation. Courtesy of the Strickland family.

Sanborn Insurance Map of 1927.[11] This allowed efficient loading of bricks within the confines of the brickyard itself for the first time in the Hudson Valley. Another of Strickland's important patented innovations—the brick shipment container—made shipping brick by rail both profitable and fast.[12] These large rectangular containers were loaded at a distance from the railroad tracks and then moved by crane onto rail cars, which allowed the trackside to remain clear the rest of the time.

Shipping brick by rail was the exception, rather than the rule, in the brick industry. Most yards either lacked proximity to the railroad or used the previously less expensive, but much slower, option of shipping by river barge. Strickland's containers solved the problem of broken bricks common to other methods of rail shipment, while at the same time increasing loading speed and efficiency, thus cutting back on man hours. By bringing the rail spur directly into the DPBW and inventing a fast, efficient method to load and contain the brick, Strickland not only made rail transport cost competitive with barge transport, but also offered much faster delivery.

Strickland's revised plant plan also included a building that appears on the Sanford Insurance map of 1927 and seems to have been a large machine shop, a power distribution center for the yard, or a building housing both these functions. Its dimensions are an impressive forty by eighty feet, with a seven-foot-thick cement foundation. It was made of brick, stone, and cement, with steel roof girders, and was of sufficient height for a second story. Indentations, supports, and a door in the middle of the wall where the second story would have begun bolster the theory that this building once had a second level. The building is still sound and has suffered little damage over the years of disuse.* It will be the first building renovated by The Beacon Institute. Research suggests that electricity was delivered to this building and then distributed to different parts of

---

* This building is presently under renovation and will serve as a visitors' center, teaching space, museum, and office space for The Beacon Institute.

the brickyard. Strickland took full advantage of electricity to upgrade the brick industry.

To help keep costs as low as possible, Strickland also effected a major change in brickyard hiring practices. "When David J. Strickland took over the management of the plant and supervision of new machinery, he adopted the policy of employing white help and made residence in Beacon one of the requirements. This policy has been followed since and the force is composed entirely of Beacon men."[13] Strickland deliberately parted from the practice of many brickyards, which involved hiring large groups of men through an agent who transported these workers from distant locations and usually without their families. Often the laborers were then housed within the bounds of the brickyard, with no ties to the surrounding community. This proved to be a recipe for disaster, both in other yards and in the early years in the DPBW. Under these circumstances life within the brickyards was dangerous and the local community scorned the workers. By requiring local residency Strickland decreased company costs by eliminating housing for workers, and also avoided the problems inherent in housing large groups of men without family ties near a strange town that was leery of people with a different racial makeup.

The racism of Strickland's policy is abhorrent, but it was commonplace at that time in our nation's history. Although black men were singled out by Strickland's discriminatory policy of hiring whites only in 1925, other ethnic groups had previously been equally disdained. In 1892 the *Fishkill Standard* reported an opinion prevalent at the time:

> The Season of Brick Making—The brickyards in this locality will shortly commence their spring operations, and the many ignorant Hungarians, Italians, etc. who usually find employment in the yards, will again be with us. The presence of these foreigners, at least the majority of them, is not at all desirable, for they are inclined to

drink and help in a large measure to support the many liquor stores in the town. They are frequently boisterous and have to be looked after with a sharp eye by the police, and often give the force much trouble and annoyance. Women and children do not care to go anywhere near them, and altogether they are an unpleasant class to have around. ... While the yards are a help to the town, many of their workmen are a curse to any civilized community.[14]

By the time Strickland implemented his whites-only hiring policy in 1925, many of these previously undesirable foreigners had blended happily into the city of Beacon, and public opinion had changed. Here, as elsewhere across America, minority groups that were successfully incorporated into communities soon forgot what it was like to be the outsiders. It appears, however, that this aspect of Strickland's policy lacked rigorous enforcement, since many of the pictures of the brickyard during his time clearly show black laborers, albeit in a minority, working alongside white men. In the end, Strickland's hiring policy made it possible for him to depend on local, and thus extremely accessible, labor without having to pay for their housing or having to wrestle with racially instigated disputes. With this policy he succeeded in raising local opinion of the brickworks to that of a desirable and positive presence in the community, rather than as merely a valuable source of revenue.

Business was excellent for the DPBW under the leadership of Strickland. The brickworks supported the New York City building frenzy that started in the late 1920s and continued through the 1930s. With its huge output of quality brick, Denning's Point was the primary brick source for many of the buildings still standing in New York City, including the Empire State Building and Rockefeller Center. In 1934 the DPBW won the contract to supply the brick to build the enormous Parkchester apartment housing complex, which provided a steady buyer for its bricks until the project's completion in 1938. "The Parkchester project, at over twelve thousand apartments,

Top: Panoramic photograph of the DPBW looking southeast from a coal silo in 1925, showing massive clay excavation area across the railroad tracks on the left, seated figure (center) at the transition point between clay-mining and brick-making operations, and the back of the drying building on the right, with seven clay-carrying railroad cars on the narrow-gauge brickyard rail line at the extreme right.

was an extraordinary accomplishment that concealed its great size by artful organization and compositions, including provision of stores, offices, a sizeable theater, and a convenient subway stop."[15] David Strickland's Jumbo brick, patented in 1934, made its debut for this project and thereafter became a staple throughout the building industry for more than twenty years. "The innovation was a simple increase of the brick height from 2¼ to 2⅝ inches, thus increasing the wall area occupied by the single brick and decreasing the

Bottom: Panoramic photograph of the clay-mining operations on the east side of the mainline railroad tracks, showing house at the top of the hill (center) that had to be moved to prevent it from sliding down the deep excavation. Photographs by Ruben. Courtesy of the Beacon Historical Society.

time required for laying a given area of wall surface."[16] The Jumbo brick became so popular that "the mason's union set a limit on the number of Jumbo bricks to be laid every day."[17] Since masons were paid by the hour, completing the job using larger bricks and taking less time resulted in lower paychecks. The union's action was intended to rectify this. Jumbo bricks continued to grow in popularity through the end of World War II and into the 1950s, but are no longer used for new construction.

*Strickland Jumbo brick, shown below a normal-sized DPBW brick for comparison.
Photograph by Jim Heron.*

Strickland's contributions to the brick industry are well documented, as is his personal story. His life exemplified the American dream. Born into a poor family in 1883, he went to work in the Haverstraw Brickyards as a teenager, instead of finishing high school. He learned quickly. By his thirtieth birthday he had progressed from merely laboring as a machine boy to designing brick machines and brickyards. He reached the height of his career during his years at the DPBW when he added to his already considerable fortune, a fortune which his family noted he shared generously with them and with his community.[18] Strickland's work ethic served as a good example to his employees, and his generosity was a boon to those who lived near Denning's Point.

Strickland took his responsibility as a citizen of Beacon seriously, and his neighbors appreciated his efforts. After only four years of residency, local citizens urged him to run for the office of mayor of

Beacon in 1929. He declined, despite a great deal of support.[19] Even without political aspirations, however, Strickland constantly looked beyond the scope of running the brickworks for other ways in which to serve the city. His community-mindedness extended to contributing to the financial stability of Beacon by assuming an instrumental role in successful negotiations to bring in a packaging facility for the National Biscuit Company, which provided the town with an additional employer. In addition, from the time Strickland took over the DPBW in 1925, he continued the trustees' policy of allowing public use of Denning's Point for recreation, and even negotiated with the city to keep the road to Denning's Point open.

Memories of public use of the Point are reflected in the personal stories of Beacon people who spent time there in the 1920s and 1930s. In an interview on August 11, 2004, Elsie Burke, now age eighty-six, recalled walking down the rail line, through the brickyards among the workers, and thence out to the point for picnics. She spoke to me of wide fields where the men played baseball and where many families shared the grounds for picnicking.

Joe "Bosh" Antalek, whose father worked in the DPBW, recounted in an interview in 2005 his daily boyhood trips through the brickyard kiln sheds on the way to the beaches at the end of the Point. He emphasized that not only were he and his companions never stopped, but the workers often joked with them as they passed on their way to the concession stands and the dancing pavilion that was open on the Point every summer. Bosh also recalled that yachts moored in the bay just off the Point and remained there for most of the summer. With a reminiscent smile he told of the big steam-driven excursion boats coming up from New York City, which threw such large wakes that he and his friends bodysurfed the waves onto the shore of Denning's Point.

The thought of bodysurfing in waters that now merely gently lap the shores of the Point intrigued me and prompted me to further research. According to eighty-four-year-old Jack Stearns, another Beaconite who spent part of his boyhood on the Point, there was an

NOW OPEN

"THE PEOPLE'S PLEASURE GROUNDS"

DENNINGS POINT

Better Than Ever Before

CLEAN, SANITARY BATH HOUSES

REFRESHMENTS

Join the Crowd at the Point!

Bath House advertisement from the Beacon Journal. *Courtesy of the Beacon Historical Society.*

James Lapis circa 1930 with his two cows beside the ruins of the Denning Mansion. Photograph courtesy of the Lapis family.

art to bodysurfing in the boats' wakes. He described at least five distinct wakes from these large steamers and told me that the secret of bodysurfing was to determine which of the wakes was the largest and then to wait patiently for it before leaping. "They [the wakes] were fairly large and, as the steamboat proceeded up or downriver, these waves, before they came ashore, would suck the water off the beaches. This action would follow the speed of the boat as she proceeded up and downriver."[20] The reputed size of the waves varied enormously, depending on the storyteller, but at least one book, *Paddle Wheel Steamers and Their Giant Engines*, substantiated the large size of the waves.[21]

Summer, for Beacon residents of all ages, officially began when the Denning's Point concessions, bathhouses, and dance pavilion opened for the season. A June 1925 advertisement from the Beacon Evening Journal was typical of the annual announcements made through 1938.

Who orchestrated the running of these concessions, changing facilities, and the dance pavilion? How did the sand that expanded the beaches beyond the natural shoreline come to be there? A 2004 interview with George Lapis, whose father Demetrius (James) Lapis emigrated to Beacon from Greece so that he could gain employment in the DPBW, shed some light on these questions. To help make ends meet, James Lapis also ran a small dairy business. In addition, the enterprising James owned and ran the concession stand and changing rooms on the Point. The *Beacon News* of June 19, 1924, proclaimed: "Jimmie has opened the refreshment stand and bath houses. Many modern improvements have been added to the equipment at the point."[22] James Lapis related to his children that the brickyard workers, at the direction of the brickyard plant manager, had mined sand from various natural sand deposits found on the Point and spread it along the western shore to provide a viable beach area for the public. It remains a mystery who was responsible for the building and running of the pavilion.

Because of the popularity of these facilities, the conditions of the roads to the Point were newsworthy details as each summer approached. An article in the June 2, 1925, *Beacon Evening Journal* noted the following:

Motorists who have traveled over the road to Denning's Point during the past week have noticed a great improvement in the condition of the road. The road has been leveled and covered with ashes and there are now few rough spots. In fact, the road is in better condition now than it has been for several years. The Byrnesville approach to the overhead bridge is in better condition than the Dennings Avenue road. This is probably due to the fact that the latter is in the city and being on the outskirts is given little attention. However, the road from Paye St. over the clay banks is in fairly good condition, much to the gratification of motorists.[23]

The article suggested that the city was somewhat remiss in keeping up the roads to the Point, while the brickworks was careful in maintaining its portion of road through the clay pits. The overstretched budget of early Beacon was satisfied by this compromise solution, and the local people recognized and appreciated the efforts of the brickworks to keep the roads to the end of Denning's Point open and safe for public use.

The DPBW proved to be an enormous economic asset to Beacon. The brickyards always closed down during the winter season, because the cost of maintaining sufficient heat for brick making was too high when the weather was cold. Before Strickland's policy dictating that workers live locally, many went home for the winters to other towns and even to other states. With the implementation of Strickland's policy, other local industries had ready access to a resident workforce during the winter months. Occasionally the DPBW also shut down for a short time during production season because brick prices or demand dropped, but operations at the brickworks always bounced back to full swing when prices rebounded or demand increased. Most of the time, the people of Fishkill Landing and Matteawan (Beacon in 1913) enjoyed the luxury of having a successful employer and a dependable business in their midst.

The brickyard's importance to the community was trumpeted in the title of an article from the January 13, 1927, edition of the Beacon Journal: "Denning's Point Brick Plant One of Beacon's Most Substantial and Beneficial Industries; $6,000 Weekly Payroll."[24] The article also pointed out that, in addition to supporting the local economy with regular paychecks, the brickworks also paid the city of Beacon thirty-one cents in tax revenue on every thousand bricks it manufactured. The brick plants in the Town of Fishkill and in other locations along the Hudson River paid taxes ranging from only eight to fourteen cents per thousand bricks. Since the DPBW was turning out 400,000 bricks a day in 1927, the DPBW's tax translated into an everyday windfall for Beacon of $124. In today's marketplace that would surpass $1,000 per day.

The DPBW even remained viable during the Depression, which meant that Beacon escaped the complete devastation suffered by many other communities in the wake of the crash of 1929, and many of the local people were able to keep working. Every family I interviewed mentioned the tents lining the river side of the Point during the early Depression years. People whose whole life-support system had disappeared sought the Point as a safe haven. Both the DPBW and the locals who viewed the Point as their playground were supportive of those hit hardest by the economic disaster. The trustees of the brickyard allowed them to camp on their property, and the locals made room. Crabbing, fishing, ball playing, and picnicking continued on the Point during the Depression years, as this 1931 *Beacon News* article highlighted:

Swimmers circa 1925. Left, beached electric boats; upper right, dance pavilion. Photograph courtesy of the Southern Dutchess Chamber of Commerce.

Hundreds Visit Denning's Point To Escape Heat: Denning's Point, now one of the most popular swimming resorts along the Hudson River, was thronged last night with several hundred bathers seeking relief from the oppressive heat. The place is ideally suited for night bathing, with its sandy and spacious beach. Powerful lights are used to illuminate both the beach and that part of the river favored by the swimmers. It was announced this morning that efforts are being made to have band concerts each Sunday afternoon with dancing to follow.[25]

By the mid-1930s, however, public use of the Point ebbed. Why this slow decline in popularity? A combination of factors contributed including increased availability of public transportation, which made vacationing away from home much more feasible, and increased interest in controlled commercial recreational ventures elsewhere. Moreover, the Point lacked year-round facilities. Then, there was the increasing pollution of the waters of the Hudson River, which certainly detracted from the charm of swimming and picnicking at the Point. Although Beacon had built a sewage treatment plant to service the east side of the city by the 1930s, in early 1940 it continued to pump raw sewage from the west side of the city directly into the Hudson, right beside Denning's Point.[26] In addition to the household sewage problem, many of Beacon's new industries disposed of chemicals, dyes, sewage, and other materials into the Fishkill Creek. This waste ended up in Denning's Point Bay.

Almost simultaneously the Denning's Point Brick Works ran into serious trouble. While the Jumbo bricks Strickland popularized were a boon for the building industry, the huge amount of clay needed to produce them exhausted the local supplies. The DPBW literally worked itself out of business and closed the industrial site on the Point in 1939. The owners of the DPBW quickly bought the property belonging to the defunct Brockway Brick Yards located about one and one-half miles north of Denning's Point. They then moved one brick-making machine and employed part of the workforce to continue production at this new site, abandoning all the rest of the industrial facilities on the Point. The famous DPBW logo remained in use, even though neither the clay nor the product was from Denning's Point.

The Denning's Point Brick Works was gone forever. Another era ended for Denning's Point, as well as for the United States of America. World War II loomed as the brickworks closed and the Point's once-proud title of "Beacon's Coney Island" faded into history. During World War II, activities on Denning's Point ceased, except for collection of materials needed for the war effort from what remained of the brickworks. The numerous metal sheds erected in the brickyard were taken as salvage, as were the steel rails from the narrow-gauge railroad and the rail spurs. Scavengers removed some of the thousands of excess bricks piled all over the Point, although many still remain.

With the end of the war in 1945, businesses looked with renewed interest at Denning's Point. Valuable riverside property never rests long before prospective owners display interest and hatch schemes for personal or business profit.

CHAPTER 8

CHANGE OF DIRECTION:
FROM INDUSTRIAL USE
TO STATE PARK

1940–1988

As I next walked around the Point, the din and busyness of the brick-yard years had melded with the other memorable times. The reverber-ations of machines and shouts of laborers had assumed their places of importance along with those of other men and women who had made history on this ground. As I trod the path following the perimeter of the Point, I noted that the only structures remaining, with the exception of the cider mill ruins and the crumbling walls of the Denning Mansion, were once part of the brickyard. They reminded me of headstones in a quiet graveyard. I looked forward to exploring the final modest industrial endeavors that followed the gigantic brickworks and preceded today's activities on this historic peninsula.

For a number of years, quiet reigned on the Point, which had been completely vacated by the end of 1939. It was still owned by the Estate of Homer Ramsdell, and David Strickland was still a prominent partner in the estate and remained so until his death in 1956. A site survey sheet filled out by archeologist Dr. Mary Butler and dated September 10, 1939, listed the name David Strickland as the person granting permission to open the archaeological dig on the Denning's Point property.[1] How many of her discoveries about the past did Dr. Butler share with Strickland, and how would he have reacted if he had known to what use the property would next be put?

The Point rapidly changed hands several times in the early 1940s. On May 1, 1942, the Estate of Homer Ramsdell sold the property to Industrial Plants Corporation. In November of that same year, Denning's Point Realty Corporation purchased the property. Then, in June of 1944, the property was purchased by four women—Anne Kriser, Marie Kriser, Virginia Danner, and Doris L. Rosenberg. History is silent about what, if anything, occurred on the Point during this period of rapid turnover in ownership. On May 19, 1947, Durisol—an independent, privately owned corporation that manufactured building materials and was headquartered in New York City—purchased the Point.

By this time the land had lain dormant for almost eight years. Beacon mourned the loss of significant tax income, and many of the local men remained unemployed. Durisol's arrival was, therefore, big news for Beacon. A front-page, eight-column banner headline in the *Beacon News* announced, "Durisol Co. Buys Denning's Point."[2] The newspaper claimed that the new owners estimated the cost of build-

Ruins of the DPBW blacksmith shop. Photograph by Jim Heron.

Remnants of the power plant building. Photograph by Patricia M. Dunne.
Courtesy of The Beacon Institute for Rivers and Estuaries.

Brickyard water heater. Photograph by Jim Heron.

The only remaining brickyard manufacturing building. Photograph by Jim Heron.

ing the new plant to be $500,000 and that they predicted employing one hundred or more workers. It quoted $60,000 as the purchase price of the Point and said it included "about 60 acres."[3]

Durisol Corporation, formed in 1946, was already operating a pilot plant in Aberdeen, Maryland, when it purchased the Denning's Point site. The Aberdeen Durisol facility remained small, housing the research and development areas and manufacturing only a minimal amount of product. The major manufacturing facility would be located on Denning's Point. Although the Durisol engineers' long-term plot plan outlined an extremely ambitious undertaking for their Beacon site, including many buildings, railroad spurs, and roads, the majority of their plans never bore fruit.[4] The plans Durisol did implement made use of existing buildings or the footprints of structures already existing on the Point. Durisol was a pioneer in the manufacture of what has become known as "green" building material because it is compatible with a healthy environment. The company consumed no natural resources from the Point and discharged no

Durisol manufacturing plant on January 4, 1949, one month before operations began. Photograph courtesy of the Library of Congress, Gottscho-Achleisner Collection.

toxins during the manufacturing process, but rather used recycled material as a primary ingredient in their final product, which contained no toxic elements.

What exactly did Durisol produce? Research shows that Durisol was not only the name of the company, but was the name of the novel product it manufactured as well. "The name 'Durisol' is derived from a combination of the French words meaning 'durable' and 'insulation.'"[5] A June 6, 1947, *Beacon News* article described the product as follows:

> Durisol is a light-weight slab of high insulation and durability having as [its] basis the use of wood fibres. These are chemically treated to render them fire resistant and termite-proof, and then mixed with cement and other ingredients resulting in a strong material combining the qualities of both wood and stone which may be sawed, cut or nailed.[6]

John Dale, president of Durisol and a native of Cold Spring, claimed that the Durisol product was ideal for sidewalls, floors, and roofs of structures. The basic Durisol material composition was developed in Switzerland in the early 1930s and was used successfully in Europe for all types of construction.[7] The Switzerland-based company registered the American patent for Durisol in 1946.

The refitting of the existing brickyard buildings was accomplished using Durisol panels manufactured in the Aberdeen plant. The new manufacturing area was 40,000 square feet with an additional 100,000 square feet used as a curing area.[8] It took more than a year to ready the facilities for operation, which began in February 1949. By mid-February of the same year, the plant boasted twenty-six employees on the payroll. Everyone held high hopes for a successful future.[9] Two months later, however, Durisol obtained a mortgage loan of $175,000 through an unnamed private institution.[10] How was Durisol able to acquire an unsecured mortgage of $175,000 on property that was purchased for $60,000 less than two years earlier? A search through Durisol's finances for the answer to this apparent discrepancy led to a series of interesting plot twists.

By 1950, just one year after starting operations on Denning's Point, Durisol employed seventy-five workers and produced 35,000 square feet of Durisol each week. In late 1950 and early 1951 the number of employees increased to one hundred; sometimes demand was so high that they worked double shifts. During this time period the company supplied materials for the IBM country club in

Interior of Durisol building. Photograph courtesy of the Library of Congress, Gottscho-Achleisner Collection.

One of the two experimental Durisol panel houses designed by Edward Durrell Stone and constructed in Garrison, New York, in the late 1940s. Photograph by Jim Heron, with the permission of the Downey family.

Poughkeepsie, the Bishop Dunn Memorial Hall at Mount St. Mary's Academy in Newburgh, and the roofs of all the restaurant franchises along the entire length of the New Jersey Turnpike. In addition it supplied roofing materials for numerous area schools and community buildings seeking to take advantage of the fire-retardant qualities of Durisol. Nearby Garrison, New York, boasts four experimental Durisol houses. The architect of two of them was Edward D. Stone, lead architect for the John F. Kennedy Center for the Performing Arts in Washington, the Museum of Modern Art in New York City, and Radio City Music Hall. As shown in the image above, the Durisol houses are quite modest, yet Durisol had sought out a famous architect as designer. The four homes are still in use and have weathered extremely well. At first glance, business appeared to be excellent, despite the need for the large mortgage loan the year before.

Two former employees of Durisol contributed to a more complete understanding of its financial picture. Paul Mara, an engineer who worked for Durisol in the Aberdeen plant and subsequently in the Beacon facility, spoke kindly of the Dale brothers who owned and managed the manufacturing plants.[11] He painted a picture of a

Durisol
PANEL
HOUSE

Architect
EDWARD STONE
Builder
J.H. WHITEHILL & SON, Inc.
Owner
ROBERT JAHN

Information
SEE LOCAL
REAL ESTATE
BROKERS
Phone LEXINGTON 2-4224 OR OAKLAND N.J. 8-5653

Original sign advertising the Durisol panel houses designed by architect Edward Durrell Stone. Photograph by Jim Heron, with the permission of the Downey family.

close-knit, intimate company that was good to its employees and for which it was easy to work. Mara noted that the company struggled from its inception to build and sustain a sales base. He opined that although the Durisol product was excellent, it was ahead of its time in the United States and, therefore, lacked the market to prosper. Betty LaColla, who worked as a secretary and the bookkeeper for Durisol from 1949 through 1952, provided more valuable information.[12] She saw Durisol workers unload railroad cars filled with cement, steel rods, and wood chips daily. The workers then loaded the same railroad cars with finished product on its way to purchasers. She also spoke of a fleet of tractor trailers bringing in raw materials and leaving loaded with finished product. In a casual comment that later turned out to be key, LaColla mentioned that Louise Boyd Dale, wife of Durisol's president John Dale, provided the capital necessary to bankroll the company.

Tony Antalek in May 1946 holding a forty-seven-pound striper just taken from the waters off the Point. Left, son Joe; right, son Jerry. Photograph courtesy of the Antalek family.

Further research uncovered a curious chain of events. A title search of the Denning's Point property revealed that on May 7, 1953, Durisol was sold to Louise Boyd Dale. Title to the property was no longer listed under the Durisol name, but under her name. Less than two weeks later, on May 16, 1953, Durisol announced its reorganization for expansion. The most intriguing part of the announcement was a quote from Thomas Dale, plant manager and brother of the president, John Dale: "Our eastern company has been reorganized. All mortgages on plant and equipment have been liquidated and the heavy unsecured debt has been eliminated. Our company is fully solvent and free of debt for the first time."[13] It was solvent and free from debt because the president's wife purchased the company and assumed all the debt! Was this sale a deliberate act to hide Durisol's indebtedness from creditors, or was it an innocent use of family money to save the company? No newspaper article mentioned this quietly accomplished sale.

Despite the Dale family's actions to keep their company afloat, the demand for Durisol remained too soft to support the manufacturing facility in Beacon. On July 24, 1954, just fourteen months after the announcement of the reorganization, Durisol closed the Beacon plant. "John Dale, president of Durisol, has confirmed that the company will cease production here. 'We cannot make money with this operation in Beacon,' he said."[14] It is an historical irony that green materials similar to those that failed to sell in the 1950s will be required for all buildings constructed for The Beacon Institute for Rivers and Estuaries on Denning's Point.

Although Durisol is now in mainstream use,[15] all that remains of the Durisol operation in Beacon are the walls and roof of the plant,

Left: Verna Ticehurst, 1943, posed on beachfront rock. Right: Verna Ticehurst, 1959, posed on same beachfront rock sixteen years later. Photographs courtesy of the Ticehurst family.

constructed with Durisol, and stacks of neatly aligned panels in several areas near the old facility. At first thought to be production refuse, these panels were actually undergoing outdoor curing—the final step of manufacture at the time the operation folded—and were simply abandoned.

Durisol's tenure on Denning's Point was less than five years. During that time the local residents continued to use the Point for recreation, but in fewer numbers and under different circumstances. Unlike their industrial predecessor, Durisol discouraged public use of the Point. According to Betty LaColla, the company was concerned with liability for injuries. This seems consistent with the specific permission granted several commercial fishermen to work from the Point as long as they carried their own insurance. Despite official policy, however, unsanctioned use of the Point by the public continued. Fishing and crabbing remained popular, with many a family meal depending on the catch.

Ticehurst family picnic with Glenn Ticehurst in the water, 1957. Photograph courtesy of the Ticehurst family.

Old-timer Elsie Burke told an amusing story of taking her children out to the end of the Point in an old jeep. Elsie explained that the men went out in advance to clean the beach of debris and oil slicks in preparation for their families' arrival. Once done with their work, the men relaxed and opened their Ballantine beer bottles as they awaited their families. From this tradition came the name by which that entire beach area became known—Ballantine Beach—and a sign soon sported the newly given name. In numerous informal interviews Gordon Ticehurst related tales of beach parties and family gatherings on the Point throughout this period, admitting that permission was never a prerequisite. He shared the pair of pictures of his wife Verna shown herein. He took one in 1943 and the other in 1959 with her sitting on exactly the same rock on the Point's southwestern beach.

Although the reversal in the open-door policy provided little deterrent to the locals during the years Durisol operated on Denning's Point, water pollution forced changes in both recreational and commercial usage. In addition to the companies that polluted the Fishkill Creek with chemical and other manufacturing toxins, large tankers and freighters rinsed their cargo holds, bilges, and water tanks directly into the Hudson River. It was a common practice for foreign vessels to travel up the Hudson just to fill their tanks with fresh water, which they transported back to their home ports as a saleable commodity. This practice constituted a dual threat. Rinsing water tanks that had been filled in their home port discharged foreign invasive organisms into the estuary, thus endangering both fish and plant life. Rinsing bilges and fuel storage tanks released petrochemicals into the water. By the early 1960s fish taken from the waters around Denning's Point were difficult to sell in the Fulton Fish Market because they tasted of diesel fuel.

Local duck hunters and shad fishermen also rued the increase in shipping waste. Fred Antalek recalled setting out white duck decoys in the early morning and returning later in the day to decoys that were dark and slimy with oil.[16] Fishermen's boats were ringed by oil

The Noesting Pin Ticket Company in the early 1970s. Photograph courtesy of the New York State Office of Parks, Recreation and Historic Preservation

lines within minutes of setting out to fish. With the shipping industry's increasingly negative impact on both commercial water ventures and recreational use, and the simultaneous closing of the Durisol manufacturing facility, what did the future hold for the Point? Ironically, another riverfront industrial facility acted as a benign buffer to additional environmental abuse.

This next chapter in the life of Denning's Point began shortly after Durisol closed in July 1954. On September 3, 1954, the *Evening News* announced that the Noesting Pin Ticket Company of New York City had purchased the Denning's Point factory at a reported price of $250,000.[17] George Frederick Griffiths Jr., president of Noesting, claimed that the transaction would be sealed on October 22 and that his firm would commence operations on Denning's Point by the end of that month. True to his word, Griffiths began manufacturing operations at the Denning's Point facility by the end of October 1954, and they continued uninterrupted for thirty-four years under the ownership of the Griffiths family.

Research into the Noesting operation soon led to the last president of Noesting, William Griffiths Sr., son of the George

Frederick Griffiths Jr. who brought Noesting to Denning's Point. William Griffiths Sr. and his son, William Griffiths Jr., answered many questions about the Noesting operation on Denning's Point in a series of face-to-face interviews and numerous phone calls. These conversations revealed that Chestnut Cove Incorporated, a holding company of the Griffiths family, was actually the new owner of the Point, rather than the Noesting Pin Ticket Company as mis-leadingly reported in the 1954 *Evening News*. Formal title only passed to Noesting on December 28, 1969, so Noesting leased the property from 1954 until its actual purchase in 1969. In 1954 the Noesting Pin Ticket Company was already a healthy corporation with offices and plants in Chicago and in the Bronx, and with warehouses in Los Angeles and in Puerto Rico. The name "Noesting" incorporates a bit of "stinging" humor. Years ago clothing prices were marked on tick-ets attached with broad, flat pins that were sharp and often pricked the fingers of salespersons and customers. Noesting came up with a better idea—a rounded-edged, "sting-less" pin ticket; hence the name, Noesting Pin Ticket Company.*

Although the people of Beacon referred to Noesting as a paper clip factory, it also manufactured pin tickets, paper fasteners, thumb tacks, hank wires,** electronic leads, commercial needles, fire extin-guisher tags, Easter egg dippers, as well as a large number of special wire creations including the crosshairs for the famous Norden bombsight. Noesting carried 400 different stock items in addition to custom products. I used one of their most successful products—a handle made of wire and wood for carrying string-tied parcels—when I worked as a wrapping clerk in my high school days. Noesting man-ufactured its own boxes and drew the wire used in its products, so it was a self-sufficient industry, which was unusual at that time.

---

* In order to insure that others pronounced the company name as No-Sting, the Griffiths added an E to make the O vowel long rather than short.
** Hank wires are four-foot-long heavy-gauge wires used by construction workers to tie reinforcing iron bars (rebar) together prior to pouring cement to stabilize it internally. Workers carried hank wires on their belts already bent in half by the manufacturer to make for quick, easy use. Since the hank wires were permanently incorporated in the structure when the cement was poured, their manufacturers reaped the benefits of the constant replacement demand.

Noesting's modest beginning turned to international success through the efforts of the Griffiths family. For the first time, products made on Denning's Point were shipped worldwide. It was another example of the American dream come true.

George Frederick Griffiths Sr., father of the George F. Griffiths Jr. who purchased Denning's Point, was a poor Welshman who emigrated to the United States in the early 1900s. He took a job as a bookkeeper with an accounting firm in New York City. When Griffiths' employer sent him to help close down a plant whose account showed imminent financial ruin, he recognized instead the facility's potential and worked out a deal with the owner to take over operations and keep it running. This newly formed industry was called Noesting Pin Ticket Company and incorporated in 1913.[18] By the time George Frederick Griffiths Sr. turned the plant over to his son, the business was flourishing, with its upper management consisting primarily of family members.

Start-up operations on Denning's Point, under the direction of George Frederick Griffiths Jr., employed ten to twenty people for the remainder of 1954, with some additions to the workforce as Noesting brought more machines on line. The workforce was made up of an approximately even number of male and female employees throughout the life of the company.

The business acumen and hands-on interest of Noesting's last president, William Griffiths Sr., son of George Griffiths Jr., contributed to the company's financial success. He bought the machines of competitors who went out of business, which made it extremely difficult for anyone else to start up a competing plant. These extra machines were stored on site in the building renovated for The Beacon Institute for Rivers and Estuaries. He also improved one of the company's machines so that it produced two hundred paper clips per minute, more than three times its previous capacity of sixty per minute. For the first twenty-five years of Noesting's tenure on the Point, business was profitable and economically stable.

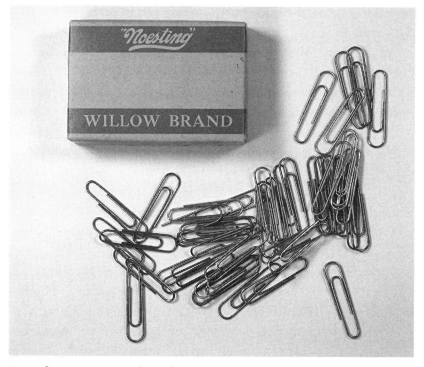

Paper clips, a Noesting product. Photograph by Patricia M. Dunne. Courtesy of The Beacon Institute for Rivers and Estuaries.

In the mid-1980s, however, Noesting lost some of its market share to overseas factories, and the viability of its Beacon factory came into question. Noesting's owner was also frustrated with the city of Beacon's failure to meet its obligation to keep in good repair the part of Denning's Point Road that led to the bridge trestle that crossed over onto the Point. When city workers finally attended to the situation, they added a right-angle turn where the bridge crossed the railroad tracks, which no large commercial truck could negotiate. In addition, representatives of Metro-North Railroad, the City of Beacon, and Noesting constantly battled over who was responsible for maintaining the railroad bridge itself. With revenue decreasing and aggravation increasing, the Griffiths were ready to consider the sale of their property, whose value had skyrocketed as developers sought to build on the riverfront.

During the years in which Noesting was in operation on Denning's Point, the public, including Noesting's last president, became increasingly aware of the importance of conservation. Environmentalists took as avid an interest in the property as developers when the business showed signs of folding. Denning's Point occupies a uniquely important ecological position: it is bounded on three sides by the Hudson River; the Fishkill Creek, a major tributary of the Hudson River, empties into its bay; it is the spawning grounds for stripers, shad, and several other species of fish; and the bulk of the Point remained intact and not yet destroyed by development or industry. The Point became a focus for both private and public environmental interests, with the State of New York, Scenic Hudson, and the Nature Conservancy speaking out regarding the need to save it from further development. Each special interest group had different ideas as to how to protect this peninsula and who should take charge, but all agreed that it *should* be preserved. Moreover, William Griffiths Sr. seemed to prefer to sell the Point to an environmentally responsible party.

The New York State Office of Parks, Recreation and Historic Preservation (NYSOPRHP) took the initiative and in August 1973 approached the president of Noesting, expressing its interest in purchasing the Point. In December 1973 NYSOPRHP put that interest in writing, and negotiations began that continued sporadically for over fifteen years. Initially those negotiations seem to have been quite civil, but they deteriorated when delineating specifics and attaching time frames to options for sale, with the unspoken possibility hanging over the Griffiths that New York State might invoke the right of eminent domain.

It was, in a way, reminiscent of the historic situation that had taken place on the same piece of land when George Washington and Alexander Hamilton had differed about how to reach their goals, although they shared a vision of what they needed to accomplish. In the modern parallel, both the Griffiths and New York State differed regarding the details of preserving Denning's Point, but both agreed that it should be done. After their initial, three-year flurry of intense negotiation, both parties seemed willing to simply wait for a mutually agreeable time to continue. The stand-off seemed more like a family squabble than an all-out war, for either side could have precipitated an ugly battle, but neither did.

The City of Beacon knew that serious negotiations to sell the Point had recommenced between the state and Noesting near the end of 1987. In a letter written on January 21, 1988, by Beacon's mayor, Vincent J. Fredericks, the city went on record as opposing the state's acquisition of the property on the grounds that the city master plan had it marked for recreational purposes. Their stance was rather baffling. As the situation stood in 1988, the fences first erected by the Durisol Corporation when it owned the property, and which were then improved upon by the Noesting Pin Ticket Company when it bought Denning's Point, legally barred local residents from recreational use of the area. Since the city wanted to use the land for a park, why not enthusiastically endorse NYSOPRHP's purchase of the property for its declared purpose of establishing a park? The state would provide the money, and the residents of Beacon would have use of a park. If, however, the city politicians were really looking at the loss in tax revenue and hoping that another industry would buy at least part of the Point, the letter made sense. The city's opposition was duly noted, but the state and Noesting continued negotiations.

In 1988 William Griffiths Sr. received an offer of over $6 million from a private developer to purchase the Point. With this offer Griffiths held the upper hand at the negotiating table; he offered the state the chance to purchase Denning's Point for a competitive amount. The state realized that it stood to lose the opportunity if it delayed, and within a few days, on October 4, 1988, it made arrangements to purchase the Point for $6 million. Everybody had won. The State of New York owns valuable parkland, and the Griffiths received a fair price for Denning's Point and delivered it into the hands of people dedicated to preserving it from inappropriate development.

Many conservation groups applauded the Griffiths' sale of the Point to the State of New York. In a press release on October 7, 1888, Orin Lehman, Commissioner of NYSOPRHP, after summarizing the importance of the purchase, thanked the Griffiths family:

> The Griffiths family, from whom the purchase was made, has demonstrated great sensitivity towards the importance of these lands to all New Yorkers. Their sense of stewardship and fairness during negotiations has made possible this significant addition to the parkland heritage of our state.[19]

At the time of its purchase, the state planned to add Denning's Point to the Hudson Highlands State Park system as simply another park in New York State's incredible collection. Concrete new evidence of the roles the Point has played in history, along with exciting new possibilities for its future, continue to emerge, however.

CHAPTER 9

From Parkland to
Promised Land
1988–Present

With Denning's Point now safe from further commercial exploitation, I felt for the first time when I next walked the perimeter that all the elements of this historic ground's varied past had come to rest in perfect harmony, united now in a communal identity. My role in the history of the Point was ending and I felt my voice slipping away to become one among the many historical voices that had been revealed during the months of research. Sadness gave way to excitement, however, when I contemplated what the future holds for Denning's Point, which now includes stewardship of the space, the resources, and of the history itself. I prepared to examine the Point's present-day condition and looked forward to participating in shaping its future.

With the purchase of Denning's Point in 1988, New York State had drawn a line in the sand that proclaimed that the environmental abuse of Denning's Point was to stop. The New York State Office of Parks, Recreation and Historic Preservation (NYSOPRHP) assumed care of the Point and linked it to the Hudson Highlands State Park system. A simple sign marked this momentous transition. Starting after its purchase and continuing through 2003, NYSOPRHP cleared and maintained a trail around the entire perimeter of the Point. Between 1988 and 2003, budget constraints prohibited all but basic maintenance and inexpensive initiatives designed to provide a modicum of convenience for hikers, bikers, picnickers, and fishermen.

While most of the park additions proved conducive to the kinds of activities NYSOPRHP wished to promote, one backfired dramatically—picnic benches placed around the Point were dragged into the remains of the industrial complex, upended, and used as protection in paint-ball battles. To add a measure of security, NYSOPRHP housed a park ranger near the entrance to the Point in the small cottage that previously served as the caretaker's cottage for both Durisol and Noesting. Establishing a ranger's residence on Denning's Point provided a visible sign of the presence of NYSOPRHP, even though the ranger's duties were primarily in other state parks.

With the advent of NYSOPRHP's proprietorship, the caretaker's role reversed completely; the job now involved inviting the public in for appropriate recreation, not warning it off. Despite its isolated location and difficult entry point, hikers, bikers, campers, birdwatchers, cross-country skiers, and fishermen made use of the park on Denning's Point, reveling on property that was legally open to the public for the first time since 1685 when the Rombout Patent was purchased from local Native Americans.

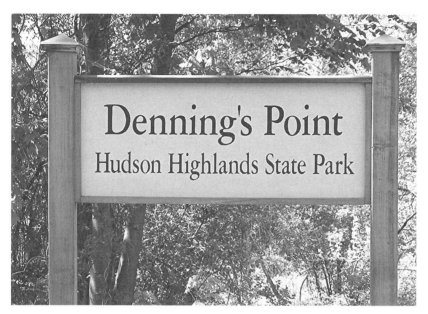

Entrance sign to Denning's Point. Photograph by Stephen Harris.

Caretaker's cottage near the entrance to Denning's Point. Photograph courtesy of New York State Office of Parks, Recreation and Historic Preservation.

In 2003 the governor of the State of New York, George E. Pataki, announced selection of Denning's Point as the site of the future Rivers and Estuaries Center—now incorporated as The Beacon Institute for Rivers and Estuaries—assuring sufficient finances, attention, and environmental protection for this once-unsung riverside park. With the placement of The Beacon Institute on Denning's Point, NYSOPRHP had a partner with whom to share the stewardship of the Point. Governor Pataki appointed John Cronin, the Hudson Riverkeeper for seventeen years, as managing director of The Beacon Institute (in April 2006 Cronin was appointed executive director). With Cronin's appointment the future began to take shape. He located the office for The Beacon Institute at 199 Main Street, right in the middle of downtown Beacon and about a mile from Denning's Point. The office opened on February 14, 2004, with one paid staff member, Patricia Dunne, in addition to John Cronin

The Rivers and Estuaries Center formally opens on February 14, 2004. Left to right: Patricia M. Dunne, program coordinator; Sister Brigid Driscoll, program manager; Vincent Tamagna, Hudson River Navigator; John Cronin, managing director; Governor George Pataki; and Mayor Clara Lou Gould of Beacon, New York.

and Sister Brigid Driscoll, who had been the coordinator of the Rivers and Estuaries Strategic Planning Committee and stayed on in the capacity of project coordinator. Initially Cronin planned to use this office as a main base until appropriate facilities could be completed on Denning's Point. The choice of the prominent site on Main Street, however, was so successful at calling attention to the ongoing project that it soon became part of the permanent overall facilities plan. The gallery-style office space invited the public to come in and to browse among the always changing exhibits, as well as to learn more about the project evolving in their own backyard. The pictorial history of Denning's Point reminded older residents of their long relationship with the peninsula and introduced younger residents to the Point for the first time. One unexpected boon of this office location was that it encouraged numerous visitors to share their personal memories of activities on Denning's Point; many of those fascinating stories are included in this book.

The staff at The Beacon Institute grew steadily as the Denning's Point facility plans moved forward. The overall project called for a multimillion-dollar scientific and educational facility covering thousands of square feet on Denning's Point. It was an exciting but complex and chaotic scene with architects, engineers, planning boards, builders, fund-raisers, and lobbyists. Endless pages of drawings appeared as the project took shape. Throughout this pandemonium, however, all concerned remained steadfastly committed to the goal that the focus of the project is on people and how to enable them to coexist happily but responsibly with the natural environment on Denning's Point over the long term. All the rest of the process—the planning and the building—is necessary, but has a limited life span. Since John Cronin was profoundly aware that intimate knowledge of the history regarding contact with the Denning's Point environment was critical as a way of coming to an understanding of the fate of other riverside communities, he knew that research and documentation of the Point's history was needed in the initial phases of the project.

The DPBW machine shop and/or its power plant (presently designated Building One by The Beacon Institute) stripped of vegetation and ready for renovation. Photograph by Jim Heron.

Architectural rendering for the exterior renovation of Building One. Courtesy of The Beacon Institute, Gensler Associates, and Margie Ruddick, landscape architect.

Building One interior in 2005. Photograph by Jim Heron.

I found soon after joining the staff as the project historian that every building and policy decision regarding The Beacon Institute is subject to consideration from the standpoint of environmental protection. The staff practices what it preaches. Their sensitivity runs the gamut from the day-to-day issues of recycling cans and using only products made with maximum recyclable material, to the more far-reaching issues of future building design and construction. Existing buildings will be restored whenever possible. When the old buildings cannot be rehabilitated, newly constructed buildings will be sited only on existing foundation footprints. Furthermore, the buildings will all be "green" buildings, designed to coexist with the ecosystem that surrounds it and manufactured from materials that were produced by environmentally sound methods. Using these criteria for construction, the transformation of the existing buildings on Denning's Point will be breathtaking.

This environmental focus extends beyond the careful planning for the actual building sites. The Beacon Institute will lease between

Architectural rendering for the interior of Building One. Courtesy of The Beacon Institute, Gensler Associates, and Margie Ruddick, landscape architect.

2005 view of the main building from the old dock. Photograph by Jim Heron.

2005 view of the interior of the main building. Photograph by Jim Heron.

eight and nine acres on the Point, including the entire industrial foot-print along with access to it. The remaining fifty-five acres will remain undeveloped parkland under the aegis of NYSOPRHP. The existing trails will stay in their current locations, but NYSOPRHP will upgrade and maintain them to encourage more use by the public.

In order to protect the American bald eagles on Denning's Point, however, the Department of Environmental Conservation, NYSO-PRHP, and The Beacon Institute jointly decided that beginning in 2005 the walking paths to the end of the Point will be closed from December 1 through March 31 each year to allow the eagles to nest and hunt without interference. Thus, even before construction began, The Beacon Institute's priorities were challenged and the staff rose to the occasion. As John Cronin exclaimed: "I love the idea that our first monitoring project on Denning's Point is going to be of the bald eagle. Our first management decision on Denning's Point is to protect the tip of Denning's Point, the southern half of Denning's Point, from human intrusion during the wintertime when bald eagles like to roost in that area."[1] How appropriate that the bald eagle, the single most enduring and universally recognizable symbol of American free-dom, will be protected where Washington rode so often during the

Revolutionary War. The American bald eagle will be safe on the very parcel of land where Hamilton penned documents whose principles were included in the United States Constitution.

Researching and documenting the Point's history provided that symbolic connection and also yielded other unexpected rewards. In the winter of 2004, NYSOPRHP contracted with John Milner Associates, Inc. for a project archaeologist to dig test pits to ensure the protection of any prehistoric artifacts that might be within the Building One site area. The footprint of the building was above suspicion, but the ground around it was suspect, given the finds of previous archaeologists. The company's project archaeologist, Geraldine Baldwin, spent several months testing different areas around the

Architectural rendering for the interior of the main building. Courtesy of The Beacon Institute, Gensler Associates, and Margie Ruddick, landscape architect.

proposed building site. The first phase of this procedure is standard for all new acquisitions of NYSOPRHP, but because of all the information that had been gathered in the writing of this book, Baldwin considered additional testing to be prudent. She found prehistoric evidence exactly where history had suggested it would be. As a result, the architects and engineers revised the plans for the underground utility corridors to avoid interference with the prehistoric cultural artifacts. Costs increased, as did the time required for construction. Decision-makers from both NYSOPRHP and The Beacon Institute, however, cooperatively implemented the necessary changes. The prehistoric sites suggested by the examination of historical documents are now permanently safeguarded.

Research on the history of Denning's Point also provided the impetus for the staff of The Beacon Institute to begin the complicated process of obtaining the state permit necessary to open a new

archaeological dig. Early in 2005, Dr. Lucille Lewis Johnson, an archaeologist on the teaching faculty of Vassar College, was contacted to assist us with the permit process and, if approval were obtained, to lead the dig. Remembering the valuable information gleaned from her predecessor's notes, it seemed appropriate to involve another archaeologist from Vassar College. Dr. Johnson agreed immediately and enthusiastically. Her expertise in negotiating the paper trail required for an archaeological excavation permit and in wading through our historical documentation resulted in the timely issuing of the desired permit. New York State maintains exacting guidelines for archaeological digs and is justifiably cautious about issuing permits. The aims of the dig for the summer of 2005 were to "check for intact prehistoric deposits on the west side of the Point where artifacts have been eroding out onto the beach, to relocate Mary Butler's site, and, time permitting, to discover whether the Denning Mansion was constructed on top of the de Peyster Mansion in which Alexander Hamilton stayed during the summer of 1781."[2]

Vassar archaeological expedition of 2005. Susan Conrad, geologist, is third from left in front row. Dr. Johnson is standing center holding a shovel, and the author is standing second from left. Photograph by Patricia M. Dunne. Courtesy of The Beacon Institute for Rivers and Estuaries.

Dr. Lucille Lewis Johnson makes history as she breaks ground on the first authorized archaeological dig on Denning's Point since 1940. Photograph by Patricia M. Dunne. Courtesy of The Beacon Institute for Rivers and Estuaries.

Dr. Johnson instructs the author in the identification of artifacts. Photograph by Patricia M. Dunne. Courtesy of The Beacon Institute for Rivers and Estuaries.

Dr. Johnson designed a summer college course for a class of thirteen students enrolled in Vassar College's Exploring Research Field Course, who carried out the archaeological dig under her direction. Susan Conrad, a geology professor from Dutchess County Community College, also joined the dig to teach the geological material, while I familiarized the students with the historical perspectives. The 2005 summer dig lasted eight days, with location parameters based on the information unearthed through my previous research. The archaeological dig conformed to meticulous excavation and record-keeping standards.

Dr. Johnson taught the group how to lay out grid squares so the location of each dig pit was precisely recorded. This was done to enable proper identification of any artifacts found, as well as to make the site easy to relocate later. The students and staff dug eighty shovel pits within these grids, which revealed 250 soil layers. After painstakingly locating each pit, the soil was removed centimeter by centimeter, screened, and the exact depth and type of soil in which any artifacts were recovered was recorded.

The care taken in a proper excavation contrasts sharply with the destructiveness of unsupervised digging in an archeological site. Archaeologically speaking, any artifacts obtained as a result of the latter are worthless, and such actions may preclude important discoveries in the future. Further, it is a crime to remove such artifacts on Denning's Point since the Point is now owned by New York State.

Denning's Point is rich in prehistoric artifacts. During the summer of 2005, a student unearthed a Bare Island point, which is a type of projectile point encountered previously in both the Booth and the Butler collections of Denning's Point artifacts. In addition to the Bare Island point, the expedition unearthed 398 flakes, fifteen chunks, six cores, four scrapers, two Rossville points, one abrader, one hammer stone, one point tip, and one ground stone tool. These discoveries reinforced the evidence of prehistoric habitation of Denning's Point. Although we tried to fulfill our objective of positive identification of the Butler archaeological dig site, it remained some-

Bare Island point found during the 2005 expedition, held in the hand of the student who uncovered it. Photograph by Edward Buhler.

what elusive. We were able to narrow the search down to one of two grids, however, one of which will be the starting point for future digs.

In efforts to meet another of the stated goals for the 2005 summer dig, we also excavated around the foundation of the Denning Mansion and found what appeared to be a second foundation and the possible site of the Hamilton residence. While further research is definitely necessary for positive identification, any proven second foundation must be dated as having been constructed in the 1700s or earlier. Whether or not the discovered foundation is that of the Hamilton residence, its presence adds important information.

Beyond meeting the stated goals for the 2005 summer dig, we also made two discoveries that answer some of the questions that remained regarding the history of Denning's Point in the years the brickyard operated. The first brickyard-related discovery came to light as a result of the auger holes Professor Conrad had her students drill to catalogue the layers and consistency of earth beneath the surface. They bored holes at two particular locations on the Point that I specified based on historical research. The first was the last spot on the Point from which the laborers in the Denning's Point Brick Works mined clay before moving east across the railroad tracks to continue their clay-mining operations. We were looking for an answer to the question of why clay mining had ceased on the Point when only one-third of the area had been tapped. Five separate auger holes along the edge of the mining line offered conclusive evidence that the clay vein had run out.

Additional auger holes, as well as some of the test pits dug along the west coast of the Point, revealed the second brickyard-related discovery. We were looking for evidence that clay had been strip-mined from the western coastline, which would explain the precipitous drop to the shoreline. Instead, we found sand on the west coast. While we knew that sand had been mined from the bay for a short time, we had no previous information proving that sand had been mined from the Point itself. With this discovery we identified both the location from which early brickyard workers mined sand, and the source from which they obtained sand to enlarge Denning's Point beaches. Because sand is prone to radical erosion, this finding explained the precipitous drop all along the western coastline. Erosion of an archaeologically sensitive site is one of the primary reasons for which the state will grant a dig permit.

Unlike the exciting archaeological dig, the building process moved along more slowly than John Cronin anticipated. He had hoped that Building One would be almost complete by the summer of 2005; however, many unexpected problems, including preserving prehistoric artifact locations, had cropped up and needed to be resolved before building could even begin. The staff of The Beacon Institute worked feverishly to keep the process moving forward, resulting in slow but steady progress. As this book goes to press, renovation of the first building is well underway.

While the actual building process has hit some snags, the vision for the future of Denning's Point remains constant under Cronin's leadership. What will Denning's Point look like when The Beacon Institute is complete, and what will be happening there in five, ten, or fifteen years? John Cronin's creative and dramatic vision of the future of Denning's Point continues to guide the joint project, stay-

Enlarged picture of Denning's Point from the north circa 1905. Left, railroad line running into the brickyard, and the extensive strip-mining along the coastline. Originally thought to be for clay mining, we now know that this coastal excavation was for sand mining. Photograph courtesy of the Beacon Historical Society.

ing the course laid out by Governor Pataki in June of 2003. Its scope includes The Beacon Institute, but encompasses more than the single site on Denning's Point. The overall plan includes cooperative research and educational facilities throughout the United States and eventually worldwide, with Denning's Point as the hub.

Cronin envisions meeting two goals within the first five years of operation of The Beacon Institute. First, he foresees all of Denning's Point, both the portion designated as parkland and the portion leased by The Beacon Institute for Rivers and Estuaries, developing an identity as the first New York State park with a completely Hudson River orientation. This new identity began to manifest itself with the eagle-monitoring program started in December of 2005. It will continue to develop as interpretive trails invite visitors to explore the complex interrelationship between the Point and the Hudson River. It will further develop as teacher-training programs expose our educators to cutting-edge environmental technology, all within the bounds of the Denning's Point environment.

Second, Cronin predicts that the research laboratory and educational facilities located in the large main building will be completely operational. The first laboratory will contain research and development facilities charged with devising advanced monitoring and

An overview of the clay-mining and sand-mining areas on Denning's Point. Sketch by Joshua Weinberg.

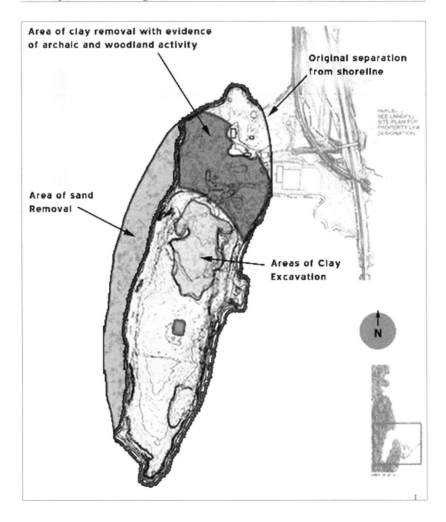

observational technologies. This facility will provide researchers at all levels, from professional down to elementary school, access to a novel source of information. Cronin explains:

> At some point school kids will be able to sit down at a computer, punch in longitude, latitude, and depth of water and actually see what is going on in the Hudson River at that very minute. They will be able to see the actual fish swimming, the contours of the bottom, the geological formations that configure the river below the water, and simultaneously see readout of chemical and physical parameters, everything from temperature to the amount of sediment that is being deposited down river. It is the researchers, policymakers, and decision makers, however, who will profit most from this incredible technology. So from Denning's Point's humble beginning we are going to see that little peninsula of land play a major role in the future of the Hudson River and in the Hudson River Estuary and by extension the rivers and estuaries of the world.[3]

In addition Cronin envisions "wiring" Denning's Point itself so that a researcher, student, or visitor can study any part of Denning's Point at any season of the year. The cameras and sensors on the land and in the waters of Denning's Point will convey such mysteries as the nesting habits of bald eagles and the spawning of shad, as they actually occur outside, to monitors inside the educational center. As the project evolves and data is added from other locations worldwide, visitors will be able to access these far-reaching phenomena from a laboratory computer monitor inside the educational center. They will experience both the excitement of a notable state park, as well as the advantages of a global center where vital information on the rivers and estuaries of the world is gathered.

Denning's Point will become a site on which all who visit may search for a more profound understanding of the world. The history of the Point, when captured in panoramic exhibits, will encourage all visitors to look deeply for connections between local and global phenomena, as well as to discern patterns as valid now as they were years ago. John Cronin talks about the unique history of Denning's Point, but notes parenthetically that if one takes any sixty-four-acre parcel of land and learns everything one can about that space, one would learn truths applicable to the rest of the world. Any parcel of land may become the context for understanding history, culture, how humans function, and how nature works. "Our goal," enthuses Cronin, "is to make sure that Denning's Point becomes an example and case history of how to do that."[4]

In the distant future John Cronin envisions the day when Denning's Point is a primary hub for a global technological network that will interconnect ongoing work from all over the United States, Europe, Asia, and the rest of the world. Researchers at Denning's Point, along with all those connected in this global network, will learn and teach others how to live with our environment better, how to manage our environment more effectively, and how to stop our environmental exploitation. All will emerge as victors if the mission of The Beacon Institute succeeds. In this far-reaching vision, our rivers and estuaries will be healthy once again. They will be able to support a revived fishing industry, function as a renewed recreational resource, and provide safer drinking water. Industrial use of the river will no longer devastate this irreplaceable resource. Cronin envisions undeveloped nations profiting enormously. How much misery caused by disease, famine, and flood might be avoided by proper management of the environment, using skills developed as a result of information gleaned in The Beacon Institute? These same acres trod by prehistoric humans, inhabited by Native Americans, settled by Europeans, figuring prominently in the American Revolution, imbued with opulence as an influential estate, and hit hard by the abuses of industrialization, now stand poised to become the focal point of change impacting the entire planet. So much may come to pass as a result of the work carried out on the sixty-four acres of Denning's Point.

Acknowledgments

A veritable legion of people gave willingly and generously of their time, talent, and personal stories to give birth to this historical and living account of Denning's Point. We share the joys of adventure, discovery, story telling, and publication.

I am deeply indebted to John Cronin, executive director of The Beacon Institute for Rivers and Estuaries, for entrusting me with this important and fascinating project and for supporting my research. Furthermore, I appreciate John's careful perusal of the manuscript and his thoughtful words in the foreword. I also gratefully acknowledge the significant contributions of the rest of the staff of The Beacon Institute, especially Patricia Dunne for her inspired photographic expertise and Regan Chichester for her wise counsel as the book developed.

To Governor George Pataki I offer my thanks for his inspired vision of a rivers and estuaries center and his support in the research and writing of this book. And to Pete Seeger, whose songs inspired my passion for justice as a young man, I am humbled that he took the time to not only read the manuscript carefully, but to offer insights that added depth to several chapters.

Without the advice and resources of the Beacon Historical Society, Denning's Point's exciting story would have remained hidden. I particularly appreciate the tireless research of its officers, Joan Van Voorhis and Bob Murphy, whose comprehensive historical knowledge of the City of Beacon was a constant guide throughout my research. Special thanks also to Spencer Barnett, deceased, who dreamed of writing this book and whose sons, John and Robert Barnett, gave me liberal access to their father's notes.

I was profoundly humbled by the patience and knowledge displayed by the personnel in the many museums, libraries, and archives; they so generously gave me access to incredible historical treasures. I am especially indebted to the personnel of the Howland

Library of Beacon, the City of Newburgh Engineering Archives, the Vassar College Library, the American Museum of Natural History, the Taiment Institute Library of NYU, the Smithsonian Institute, the Museum of the American Indian, and the New York State Museum. I am deeply grateful to Andrea Lain, archaeology collections manager of the NYS Museum, for her patient explanations of artifacts and invaluable gift of time.

The New York State Department of Parks, Recreation and Historical Preservation was truly extraordinary as it strove to make accessible every possible person, file, or picture that was even remotely connected to Denning's Point. I am especially appreciative of the enthusiastic support of Jim Moogan, deputy commissioner of operations for the Hudson Valley, Ken Lutters, senior landscape architect Taconic Region, and Anne Cassidy, collections manager.

It would take another book to name each of my fellow Beaconites who shared a personal story or two as well as those of their ancestors. You know who you are, so let me simply say, "Thank you all" from the bottom of my heart. I also extend deep-seated gratitude to Susan Strickland and David Murphy for their insights and information about their grandfather, David Strickland, who played such an important role in the history of Denning's Point. Thank you William Griffiths for spending hours with me relating the previously untold story of the Noesting Pin Ticket Company.

My sincere thanks to Linda Wood, longtime friend and first reader extraordinaire, who saw the statue within the uncut stone of my prose and who, just maybe, cured me of abusing the passive voice in my writing. And to Dr. Lucille "Lucy" Lewis Johnson, whose archaeological expertise in leading the expedition of 2005 was excelled only by her willingness to share her knowledge and her friendship by including me as staff on the first dig on Denning's Point in over sixty years.

Finally, I am deeply appreciative of all the unsung heroes who worked between the covers of this book by separating the chaff from the wheat and gently guiding me through the incredible process of "putting a book to bed." To each and every one I extend a special thank you. *Muchas gracias* to my proofreaders Matina Billias and Natalie Mortensen for their expertise in identifying errors and improving the flow of the text. *Merci beaucoup* to Ron Toelke and Barbara Kempler-Toelke for their gift of capturing the aura of Denning's Point in the cover design and the layout of the entire book. *Vielen Dank* to Deborah Allen, publisher of Black Dome Press, for believing in the story of Denning's Point and taking a risk with this first-time author. *Grazie mille* to my editor, Steve Hoare, for his careful and thoughtful editing, but even more so for his willingness to enter into the story of Denning's Point; he refined this book in so many essential ways. The vision and guidance of both Deborah and Steve shaped this story and polished the many rough edges so that you, the reader, would be captivated as I was by the unfolding story of Denning's Point. They turned my dream into a reality.

Notes

Introduction

1. Press Release. Office of the Governor, State of New York, "Governor Announces Plan for Rivers and Estuaries Center," albany, New York, July 31, 2001.

Chapter 1—In Search of the Beginning

1. Henry Noble MacCracken, *Old Dutchess Forever* (New York: Hastings House, 1956), 3.
2. "Sites of Old Indian Villages and Cemeteries are Located In County," *Beacon News,* (Beacon, NY), February 1, 1930.
3. MacCracken, *Old Dutchess Forever,* 2.
4. Mary Butler, "A Hudson Valley Archaeological Survey, 1939–40" [ca. September 1940], Butler Collection, Archives of the New York State Museum, Albany, New York.
5. Ibid.
6. Arthur C. Parker, *The Archaeological History of New York, Part 2: New York State Museum Bulletin Nos. 237–238* (Albany, NY: The University of the State of New York, September–October 1920), 548.
7. William M. Beauchamp, *The Aboriginal Occupation of New York, New York State Museum Bulletin No 32, Vol 7* (Albany, NY: The University of the State of New York, February 1900), 60.
8. Ibid.
9. "Antiquities of Onondaga, Vol. 5, 1893" (Albany, NY: unpublished manuscript in the New York State Library Manuscripts and Special Collections), 10–13.
10. Ibid., 10–11.
11. MacCracken, *Old Dutchess Forever,* 2.
12. Henry Booth, "Letter to William Beauchamp," The Papers of Henry Booth, American Museum of Natural History, New York, 1908.
13. Beauchamp, "Antiquities of Onondaga," 12.
14. William A. Ritchie, *The Archaeology of New York State* (Garden City, NY: The Natural History Press, 1965), 1.
15. Robert E. Funk, *Recent Contributions to Hudson Valley Prehistory. New York State Museum Memoir 22* (Albany, N.Y.: The University of the State of New York, 1976), 306.
16. Ritchie, *The Archaeology of New York State,* op cit., 1
17. Office of the State Archaeologist, *Major Aboriginal Projectile Points in New York State,* (Albany, NY: New York State Museum press).
18. Ritchie, *The Archaeology of New York State,* 31.
19. Ibid., 91.
20. E.M. Ruttenber, *Indian Tribes of Hudson's River to 1700,* a facsimile reprint of the original 1872 edition, (Saugerties, NY: Hope Farm Press & Bookshop, 1992), 85.

21. Ibid., 42.
22. Ibid., 42–43.
23. Frank Hasbrouck, *History of Dutchess County New York* (Poughkeepsie, NY: S.A. Matthieu Press, 1909), 24.

Chapter 2—The Early Years

1. James H. Smith, *1683 History of Dutches County New York* (Interlaken, NY: Heart of the Lakes Publishing, 1980), 40.
2. *Henry Hudson and the Dutch in New York* (Albany, NY: University of the State of New York, State Education Department, 1964), 28.
3. E.M. Ruttenber, *Indian Tribes of Hudson's River to 1700*, a facsimile reprint of the original 1872 edition, (Saugerties, NY: Hope Farm Press & Bookshop 1992), 7.
4. Ibid., 8.
5. *Henry Hudson and the Dutch in New York*, 29.
6. Ruth B. Polhill, "Through the Years," *Souvenir Program: Beacon Golden Jubilee* (Beacon, NY: Beacon Free Press, 1963).
7. William Willis Reese, *Eighteenth Century Records of the portion of Dutchess County New York that was included in ROMBOUT PRECINCT and the original TOWN of FISHKILL* (Poughkeepsie, NY: Collections of the Dutchess County Historical Society, Volume VI, 1938), 6.
8. Frank Hasbrouck, *History of Dutchess County New York* (Poughkeepsie, NY: S.A. Matthieu Press, 1909), 323.
9. Henry D.B. Bailey, *Local Tales and Historical Sketches* (Fishkill Landing, NY: John W. Spaight, Publisher, 1874), 293.
10. Ibid., 315.
11. *The Indian deed of sale to Francis Rombout and Gulian Verplanck* (Albany, NY: Records of the Secretary of State, Book of Patents, 5:206, 1683).
12. Henry Cassidy, *The Rombout Patent* (Poughkeepsie, New York: Dutchess County Historical Society, 1985), 4.
13. Hasbrouck, *History of Dutchess County New York*, 37.
14. Ruttenber, *Indian Tribes of Hudson's River to 1700*, 26.
15. Researching the forms of government among the Native Americans and studying the negotiations they conducted with the agents of Rombout and Verplanck led to an increasing respect for the native people on my part, but what was the opinion of their white contemporaries? I found this quirky, but related, piece of information: "De La Rasieres, the earliest writer, 1628, thought the Indians 'of an orange color, like the Brazilians.' Hudson had called them swarthy. A friend of Governor Kieft called them 'of ordinary stature, strong and broad-shouldered; olive colored, light and nimble on foot, subtle of mind, of few words which they previously well consider, hypocritical, treacherous, vindictive, brave and obstinate in self-defense, in time of need right resolute to all.' This was written after Kieft's war upon the Indians, when the white men far outdid the savages in the ill qualities. Van Der Donck of Yonkers called the Indians 'yellow, as yellow as the people who sometimes pass through the Netherlands and are called gypsies.' The Iroquois called themselves brown, as the Dutch reported. Verrazano the Italian thought them lighter than his countrymen. One color they never

thought of: red. The term 'redskin' is not quoted from English or American sources before 1790." Henry Noble MacCracken, *Old Dutchess Forever* (New York: Hastings House, 1956), 4.

16. Ibid., 66.
17. Henry Cassidy, *Catharyna Brett: Portrait of a Colonial Businesswoman* (Poughkeepsie, NY: Dutchess County Historical Society Yearbook, Vol 77, 1992), 35.
18. Smith, *1683 History of Duchess County*, 60.
19. Spencer Barnett, "Denning's Point–An Enclave of History" an unpublished paper, Beacon Historical Society Archives, ND.
20. MacCracken, *Old Dutchess Forever*, 73.
21. Cassidy, *Catharyna Brett*, 105.
22. MacCracken, *Old Dutchess Forever*, 66.
23. Ibid., 65.
24. Waldron Phoenix Belknap Jr., *The de Peyster Genealogy* (Boston: privately printed, 1956), 13.
25. Cassidy, *Catharyna Brett*, 105.

Chapter 3—The Revolutionary War Period

1. Rodney McDonough, "William Denning," *New York Genealogical and Biographical Record, vol. xxx, No.3* (New York, July, 1899), 133.
2. Ibid., 133.
3. Ibid., 134.
4. US Printing Office, "William Denning," *Biographical Directory of the American Congress 1774–Present.* http://bioguide.congress.gov/scripts/biodisplay.pl?index=D000240.
5. MacDonough, *New York Genealogical and Biographical Record*, 136.
6. Ibid., 138.
7. Ibid.
8. John C. Fitzpatrick, ed., *The Writings of George Washington, Volume 20* (United States Government Printing Office, Washington, D.C., 1937), 283.
9. Ibid., 413.
10. McDonough, New York *Genealogical and Biographical Record*, 138.
11. Ibid.
12. "Fishkill in the Revolution," *Fishkill Standard* (Fishkill-on-the-Hudson, NY), April 8, 1876.
13. "The Washington Oaks," *Fishkill Standard* (Fishkill-on-the-Hudson, NY), April 30, 1881.
14. A March 12, 1870, article in the *Fishkill Standard* tells of William H. Denning counting the rings in a fallen oak that measured thirteen feet in circumference. Seven hundred rings were counted, "making its age that number of years." The article also noted that the companion oak to the fallen one measured eighteen feet in circumference, suggesting an age of over one thousand years.
15. Harold C. Syrett, ed., *Papers of Alexander Hamilton* (New York: Columbia University Press, 1961), Volume II:1779–1781, 558.
16. Ibid., Volume III, 644.

17. Ibid., Volume III, 671–672.
18. Ibid., Volume IV, 150–153.
19. Ibid., Volume XVI, 59.
20. Ibid., Volume X11, 425.
21. Ibid., Volume II, page 566.
22. Broadus Mitchell, "Hamilton's Quarrel with Washington, 1781," *William and Mary Quarterly* (April 1955), 199–216.
23. Ron Chernow, *Alexander Hamilton* (New York: Penguin Press, 2004), 154.
24. Ibid., 606.
25. Ibid., 635.
26. James Thomas Flexner, *The Young Hamilton: A Biography* (New York: Fordham University Press, 1997), 342.
27. Ibid., 343.

Chapter 4—The Glory Years

1. Henry Noble MacCracken, *Blythe Dutchess* (New York: Hastings House, 1958), 247.
2. Ibid.
3. Helen Wilkinson Reynolds, *Dutchess County Doorways and Other Examples of Period-Work in Wood, 1730–1830* (New York: William Farquar Payson, publisher, 1931), 43–44.
4. MacCracken, *Blythe Dutchess*, 249.
5. Reynolds, *Dutchess County Doorways and Other Examples of Period-Work in Wood, 1750–1880*, 44.
6. Frank Hasbrouck, *History of Dutchess County New York* (Poughkeepsie, NY: S.A. Matthieu Press, 1909), 299.
7. William S. Pelletreau, *A History of Putnam County, New York* (Philadelphia: W.W. Preston & Co., 1886), 529.
8. Ibid., 526.
9. J.R. Van Rensselaer, "Recollections of Presqu'ile by Mrs. J.R. Van Rensselaer [ca. 1898], Archives of the Beacon Historical Society, Beacon, New York.
10. Ibid.
11. Ibid.
12. Ibid.
13. Ibid.
14. "Sloop Sunk," *Fishkill Standard* (Fishkill-on-the Hudson, NY), June 14, 1866.
15. Van Rensselaer, *Recollections of Presqu'ile by Mrs. J.R. Van Rensselaer.*
16. Ibid.
17. Ibid.
18. Ibid.
19. William H. Denning to Governor Hamilton Fish, 10 December 1849. Archives of the Beacon Historical Society, Beacon, New York.
20. "Cider Making," *Fishkill Standard* (Fishkill-on-the-Hudson, NY), December 7, 1872.
21. Van Rensselaer, *Recollections of Presqu'ile by Mrs. J.R. Van Rensselaer.*
22. "Weather," *Fishkill Standard* (Fishkill-on-the-Hudson, NY), February 1, 1866.
23. "Some Reminiscences of Nearly Forty Years Ago." *Fishkill Standard* (Fishkill-on-the-Hudson, NY), December 25, 1897.

24. "The Denning Guard," *Fishkill Standard* (Fishkill-on-the-Hudson, NY), January 2, 1931.
25. Ibid.
26. James H. Smith, *1683 History of Dutchess County, New York* (Interlaken, NY: Heart of the Lakes Publishing, 1980), 511.
27. Virginia Hughes Kaminsky, ed., *A War to Petrify the Heart: The Civil War Letters of a Dutchess County, N.Y. Volunteer* (Hensonville, N.Y.: Black Dome Press, 1997), 39.
28. "Denning Guard," *Fishkill Standard* (Fishkill-on-the-Hudson, NY), October 6, 1877.
29. Dan Liebman, "Convergence: The Story Behind a Photograph" (term paper, Haverford College, PA, 1963), 18.
30. "First Parade," *Fishkill Standard* (Fishkill-on-the-Hudson, NY), Nov 24, 1896.
31. "Died,"

Chapter 5—The Decline and Fall of the Glory Years

1. Charles Caldwell, Survey Field Book No 92, June 1879, Newburgh Engineering Archives, Newburgh, NY) 30.
2. "Presqu'ile," *Fishkill Standard* (Fishkill-on-the-Hudson, NY), September 21, 1918.
3. "BH & E Railroad," *Poughkeepsie Eagle* (Poughkeepsie, NY), June 10, 1869.
4. Bernard L. Rudberg, *Twenty-Five Years on the ND&C* (Fleischmanns, NY: Purple Mountain Press, 2002), 71.
5. *Emily Van Rensselaer & Jane L. Denning v The Boston, Hartford and Erie Railroad Company* (Supreme Court, County of Dutchess, Poughkeepsie, NY, 1870), 1.
6. "The Denning Point Property," *Fishkill Standard* (Fishkill-on-the-Hudson, NY), December 3, 1870.
7. Caldwell, *Survey Field Book No 92*, 30–31.
8. "145 Men Make 300,000 Soft Mud Bricks Daily," *Brick and Clay Record* (Chicago, IL, Cahners Publishing Company, August, 1927), 322.
9. "The Denning Point Property," *Fishkill Standard* (Fishkill-on-the-Hudson, NY), March 4, 1871.
10. "Valuable Property at Auction," *Fishkill Standard* (Fishkill-on-the-Hudson, NY), April 27, 1872.
11. "Foreclosure Sale," *Fishkill Standard* (Fishkill-on-the-Hudson, NY), May 11, 1872.
12. Walter Barrett, *The Old Merchants of New York City* (New York: Carleton Publisher, 1813), 50–51.
13. "Presqu'ile," *Fishkill Standard* (Fishkill-on-the-Hudson, NY), September 21, 1918.
14. J.R. Van Rensselaer, "Recollections of Presqu'ile by Mrs. J.R. Van Rensselaer [ca. 1898]," Archives of the Beacon Historical Society, Beacon, New York.
15. "Denning's Point," *Fishkill Standard* (Fishkill-on-the-Hudson, NY), August 3, 1889.
16. "The Old Denning Mansion," *New York Times* (New York), January 4, 1890.

Chapter 6—The Early Years
of the Denning's Point Brick Works: 1880–1920

1. "Trespassing upon Denning's Point," *Fishkill Standard* (Fishkill-on-the-Hudson, NY), September 22, 1877.
2. "Another Brickyard in Fishkill," *Poughkeepsie Eagle* (Poughkeepsie, NY), August 11, 1880.

3. Ibid.
4. "The Mammoth Brickyard," *Fishkill Standard*, October 23, 1880.
5. "The Denning's Point Brickyard," *Fishkill Standard*, March 26, 1881.
6. "Finding Relics," *Fishkill Standard*, April 2, 1881.
7. "Tioronda," *Fishkill Standard*, June 7, 1890.
8. George V. Hutton, *The Great Hudson River Brick Industry* (Fleischmanns, NY: Purple Mountain Press, 2003), 71.
9. "The New Brickyard at Denning's Point," *Fishkill Standard*, April 30, 1881.
10. Charles Ellery Hall, *The Story of Brick* (New York : Building Trades Employers' Association Bulletin, 1905), 25.
11. "The Mammoth Brickyard," *Fishkill Standard*, April 30, 1881.
12. Hall, *The Story of Brick*, 25.
13. "Expert Thieves Along the Hudson," *New York Times*, Nov 3, 1877.
14. "Attempt to Wreck a Brickyard," *Newburgh Journal* (Newburgh, NY), May 12, 1891.
15. Ibid.
16. "The Obituary Record: Homer Ramsdell," *New York Times* (New York), February 14, 1894.
17. "Homer Ramsdell Dead," *Newburgh Journal*, (Newburgh, NY), February 13, 1894.
18. "Funeral of Homer Ramsdell," *Newburgh Journal*, February 16, 1894.
19. "Fishkill's Coney Island," *Fishkill Standard*, August 11, 1900.
20. "The Perils of Picnicing [sic] at Denning's Point," *Fishkill Standard*, July 14, 1900.
21. Ibid.
22. "How Squaws Spent Spare Time," *Newburgh Daily News*, June 29, 1915.
23. Ibid.
24. "Caring for the Inner Man at Canoeists Camp," *Newburgh Daily News*, July 3, 1915.
25. "Point Almost Deserted," *Newburgh Daily News*, June 29, 1915.
26. "Canoeists' Outing Ends," *New York Times*, July 6, 1915.
27. "Down by Denning's Point," *Fishkil Standard*, May 7, 1904.

Chapter 7—The Peak and Collapse of the Brick Works: 1920–1940

1. "145 Men Make 300,000 Soft Mud Bricks Daily," *Brick and Clay Record* (Chicago, IL. (Cahners Publishing Company, August, 1927), 322.
2. "Tons of Clay in Landslide at Brickyard," *Beacon Evening Journal* (Beacon, NY), August 23, 1923.
3. "Low Output is Cause of Brick Strike," *Beacon Evening Journal* (Beacon, NY), May 18, 1925.
4. George V. Hutton, *The Great Hudson River Brick Industry* (Fleischmanns, NY: Purple Mountain Press, 2003), 72.
5. "Plan to Clean up Brickyard is Undertaken," *Beacon Evening Journal* (Beacon, NY), December 1, 1926.
6. Ibid.
7. "Man Pleads Not Guilty to Murder," *Poughkeepsie Star–Enterprise* (Poughkeepsie, NY), June 18, 1937.
8. "145 Men Make 300,000 Soft Mud Bricks Daily," *Brick and Clay Record*, 322.
9. Ibid., 322

10. "Denning's Point Brick Works Goes on Double Shift Monday: Record Production Expected," *Beacon Journal* (Beacon, NY), May 25, 1927.
11. Hutton, *The Great Hudson River Brick Industry*, 151.
12. Ibid., 151.
13. "Denning's Point Brick Plant One of Beacon's Most Substantial and Beneficial Industries 6,000 Weekly Payroll," *Beacon Evening Journal* (Beacon, NY), January 13, 1927.
14. "The Season of Brick Making," *Fishkill Standard* (Beacon, NY), April 9, 1892.
15. Hutton, *The Great Hudson River Brick Industry*, 157.
16. Ibid., 157–158.
17. Ibid., 158.
18. David Murphy [grandson of David Strickland], letter to the author. July 3, 2004.
19. "Strickland Is Mentioned For The Mayorality," *Beacon News* (Beacon, NY), June 20,1929.
20. Jack Stearns, in a telephone conversation with the author, September 22, 2005.
21. Bob Whittier, *Paddle Wheel Steamers and Their Giant Engines* (Duxbury, Mass.: Seamaster Press, 1987), 29.
22. "Warm Weather Brings Crowds to the Point," *Beacon News* (Beacon, NY), June 19, 1924.
23. "Denning's Point Road Is In Good Condition," *Beacon Evening Journal* (Beacon, NY), June 6, 1925.
24. "Denning's Point Brick Plant One of Beacon's Most Substantial and Beneficial Industries $6,000 Weekly Payroll," *Beacon Journal* (Beacon, NY), January 13, 1927.
25. "Hundreds Visit Denning's Point To Escape Heat," *Beacon News* (Beacon, NY), July 30, 1931.
26. "State Board Gives Village 5-Year Respite," *Beacon News* (Beacon, NY), July 13, 1940.

Chapter 8—Change of Direction:
from Industrial Use to State Park: 1940–1988

1. Archaeological work notes of Mary Butler, Ph.D., June and July 1940, Butler Collection, NYS Museum Archives, Albany, New York.
2. "$500,000 Plant to Employ 100," *Beacon News* (Beacon, NY), June 6, 1947.
3. Ibid.
4. Alexander D. Crosett's Plot Plan for the Durisol Company, September 1947, Durisol Archives, New York State Office of Parks, Recreation and Historic Preservation, Staatsburg, NY.
5. "New Type Building Material Produced At Durisol Plant," *Beacon News* (Beacon, NY), September 22, 1950.
6. "$500,000 Plant to Employ 100," *Beacon News* (Beacon, NY), June 6, 1947.

7.   "New Type Building Material Produced At Durisol Plant," *Beacon News*, September 22, 1950.

8.   Ibid.

9.   "Durisol Plant to Begin Operations January 17," *Beacon News*, January 8, 1949.

10. "Durisol Gets $175,000 Loan," *New York Times* (New York), April 4, 1949.

11. Paul Mara, in a telephone conversation with the author, May 8, 2005.

12. Betty LaColla, in two telephone conversations with the author, May 8, 2005, and June 10, 2005.

13. "Reorganize Durisol for Expansion," *Beacon News* (Beacon, NY), May 16,1953.

14. "Durisol Plant Closes; To Offer Site For Sale," *Beacon News* (Beacon, NY), July 24, 1954.

15. While searching for additional information about the Durisol produced on Denning's Point, I contacted the present-day Durisol main office in Ontario, Canada, which immediately forwarded my inquiries to Hans J. Rerup, the chief executive officer and owner of Durisol. To my great surprise he stated categorically that Durisol never had a manufacturing facility in Beacon or in Aberdeen. I assured him that I had proof of the existence of a substantial Durisol plant in Beacon in the form of newspaper articles, county court records, and detailed engineering plans for the entire facility. Furthermore, I pointed out that the Durisol he was producing used the same patented material produced in the Beacon plant and I cited the patent number and patent holder. Even Rerup's contacts in the Swiss parent company claimed ignorance of the Durisol operation on Denning's Point. There is, however, no doubt that Durisol in Beacon was a precursor of present-day Durisol. Durisol is presently successfully producing sound baffles for super highways, including the New York State Thruway, and building panels for large construction projects, including the twenty-five-story Hilton Inn in Windsor, Canada.

16. Frederick Antalek, in an interview with the author, July 15, 2005.

17. "Noesting Company Buys Denning's Point Factory," *Evening News* (Beacon, NY), September 3, 1954.

18. "New Incorporations," *New York Times* (New York), July 10, 1913.

19. Orin Lehman, press release from the New York State Office of Parks, Recreation and Historic Preservation, October 7, 1988.

Chapter 9—From Parkland to Promised Land: 1988–Present

1.   John Cronin, in an interview with the author, October 25, 2005.

2.   Lucy Lewis Johnson, Ph.D. Report to the New York State Museum on Archaeological Testing at Denning's Point, Beacon, NY, summer 2005.

3.   John Cronin, in interviews with the author, November 5 and November 30, 2005

4.   Ibid.

Bibliography

Bailey, Henry D.B. *Local Tales and Historical Sketches*. Fishkill Landing, N.Y.: John W. Spaight, Publisher, 1874.

Barrett, Walter. *The Old Merchants of New York City*. New York: Carleton Publisher, 1813.

Beacon Historical Society Archives. "Recollections of Presqu'ile by Mrs. Van Rensselaer [ca. 1898]." Archives of the Beacon Historical Society, Beacon, New York.

———. William H. Denning to Governor Hamilton Fish, 10 December 1849. Archives of the Beacon Historical Society, Beacon, New York.

Beauchamp, William M. *The Aboriginal Occupation of New York. New York State Museum Bulletin No. 32, Vol. 7*. Albany, N.Y.: The University of the State of New York, 1900.

———. "Antiquities of Onondaga, Vol. 5, 1893," Albany, N. Y.: New York State Library Manuscripts and Special Collections, 1893.

Belknap, Waldron Phoenix. *The de Peyster Genealogy*. Boston: privately printed, 1956.

Booth, Henry. The Papers of Henry Booth. American Museum of Natural History, New York. 1908.

Brick and Clay Record. "145 Men Make 300,000 Soft Mud Bricks Daily." The Brick and Clay Record (August 1927): 322–335.

Butler Collection. Archives of the New York State Museum, Albany, New York.

Caldwell, Charles. Newburgh Engineering Archives, Newburgh, N.Y.

Cassidy, Henry. *The Rombout Patent*. Poughkeepsie, N.Y.: Dutchess County Historical Society, 1985.

———. *Catharyna Brett, Portrait of a Colonial Businesswoman: Dutchess County Historical Society Yearbook Vol. 77*. Poughkeepsie, N.Y.: Dutchess County Historical Society, 1992.

Chernow, Ron. *Alexander Hamilton*. New York: The Penguin Press, 2004.

Fitzpatrick, John C., ed. *The Writings of George Washington: from the Original Manuscript Sources 1745–1799. 39* Volumes. Washington, D.C.: United States Government Printing Office, 1937.

Flexner, James Thomas. *The Young Hamilton: A Biography.* New York: Fordham University Press, 1997.

Funk, Robert E. *Recent Contributions to Hudson Valley Prehistory. New York State Museum Memoir 22.* Albany, N.Y.: The University of the State of New York, 1976.

Hall, Charles Ellery. *The Story of Brick.* New York: Building Trades Employers' Association, 1905.

Hasbrouck, Frank. *History of Dutchess County New York.* Poughkeepsie, N.Y.: S.A. Matthieu Press, 1909.

Hutton, George V. *The Great Hudson River Brick Industry.* Fleischmanns, N.Y.: Purple Mountain Press, 2003.

Kaminsky, Virginia Hughes, ed. *A War to Petrify the Heart: The Civil War Letters of a Dutchess County, NY Volunteer.* Hensonville, N.Y.: Black Dome Press, 1997.

Liebman, Dan. "Convergence: The Story Behind a Photograph." Term Paper, Haverford College, Penn., 1963.

MacCracken, Henry Noble. *Blythe Dutchess.* New York: Hastings House, 1958.

————. *Old Dutchess Forever* New York: Hastings House, 1956.

McDonough, Rodney. "William Denning." *New York Genealogical and Biographical Record, vol. xxx, No.3* (July 1899):133–141.

Mitchell, Broadus. "Hamilton's Quarrel with Washington, 1781." *William and Mary Quarterly* (April 1955): 199 –216.

O'Connor, Richard P. "A History of Brickmaking in the Hudson Valley." Ph.D. diss., University of Virginia, 1987.

Parker, Arthur C. *The Archaeological History of New York. New York State Museum Bulletin Nos. 237, 238.* Albany, N.Y.: The University of the State of New York, 1920.

Pelletreau, William S. *A History of Putnam County, New York.* Philadelphia: W.W. Preston & Co., 1866.

Polhill, Ruth B. *Souvenir Program: Beacon Golden Jubilee*. Beacon, N.Y.: Beacon Free Press, 1963.

Pollan, Michael. *The Botany of Desire*. New York: Random House, 2001.

Reese, William Willis. *Eighteenth Century Records of the Portion of Dutchess County New York that was included in Rombout Precinct and the original Town of Fishkill*. Poughkeepsie, N.Y.: Collections of The Dutchess County Historical Society, Volume VI, 1938.

Reynolds, Helen Wilkinson. *Dutchess County Doorways and Other Examples of Period-Work in Wood*. New York: William Farquhar Payson, 1931.

Ritchie, William A. *The Archaeology of New York State*. Garden City, N.Y.: The Natural History Press, 1965.

Rudberg, Bernard L. *Twenty-Five Years on the ND & C*. Fleischmanns, N.Y.: Purple Mountain Press, 2002.

Ruttenber, E.M. *Indian Tribes of Hudson's River to 1700*. 1872. Reprint, Saugerties, N.Y.: Hope Farm Press & Bookshop, 1992.

Smith, James H. *History of Dutchess County, New York: 1683–1882*. 1882. Reprint, Interlaken, N.Y.: Heart of the Lakes Publishing, 1980.

State of New York. *The Indian Deed of Sale to Francis Rombout and Gulian Verplanck*. Albany, N.Y.: Records of the Secretary of State, Book of Patents, 5:206, 1683.

Syrett, Harold C., ed. *The Papers of Alexander Hamilton*. 27 volumes. New York: Columbia University Press, 1961.

United States Printing Office. "William Denning." *Biographical Directory of the American Congress 1774–Present*. http://bioguide.congress.gov/scripts/biodisplay.pl?index=D00020.

University of the State of New York. *Henry Hudson and the Dutch in New York*. Albany, N.Y.: State Education Department, 1964.

Whittier, Bob. *Paddle Wheel Steamers and Their Giant Engines*. Duxbury, Mass.: Seamaster Press, 1987.

Index

ABOUT THE AUTHOR

Jim Heron lives in Beacon, New York, where he is project historian for The Beacon Institute for Rivers and Estuaries. He received a Bachelor of Arts degree in English from Norwich University, a Masters in Sacred Theology from the Episcopal Divinity School, and a Doctorate in Ministry from Drew University.

Heron taught at the Trinity Pawling School, was director of the Diocesan School for Deacons in the Episcopal Diocese of New York, and was adjunct professor at Drew University. He was a 9/11 Ground Zero chaplain and the founding president of Hospice of Dutchess County. He retired in 2003 after thirty-eight years in the priesthood, the last twenty-three years as Rector of Trinity Episcopal Church in Fishkill, New York. He has two children, a son Tim and a daughter Megan.

Heron's eclectic interests include photography, mineralogy, baseball, motorcycles, and creating scroll saw art. In rare moments when he relaxes completely, Heron may be found in front of a glowing fire, mystery novel in hand, contemplating Sin (his ash-gray cat, Sinders), and anticipating his next project.